D0235585

I Want My Mummy Back

I Want My Mummy Back

A Moving True Story of One
Family's Loss

JON NICHOLSON

LONDON

1 3 5 7 9 10 8 6 4 2

Published in 2008 by Vermilion, an imprint of Ebury Publishing

Ebury Publishing is a Random House Group company

Copyright © Jon Nicholson 2008

Jon Nicholson has asserted his right to be identified as the author of this Work in accordance with the Copyright, Designs and Patents Act 1988.

The Random House Group Limited Reg. No. 954009

Addresses for companies within the Random House Group can be found at
www.rbooks.co.uk

A CIP catalogue record for this book is available from the British Library

Mixed Sources
Product group from well-managed
forests and other controlled sources
www.fsc.org   Cert no. TT-COC-2139
© 1996 Forest Stewardship Council

The Random House Group Limited supports The Forest Stewardship Council (FSC), the leading international forest certification organisation. All our titles that are printed on Greenpeace approved FSC certified paper carry the FSC logo. Our paper procurement policy can be found at www.rbooks.co.uk/environment

Printed and bound in the UK by CPI Mackays, Chatham ME5 8TD

ISBN 978 0 09 192373 0

Copies are available at special rates for bulk orders. Contact the sales development team on 020 7840 8487 for more information.

To buy books by your favourite authors and register for offers, visit
www.rbooks.co.uk

This is for my children, Molly, Maisy and Sam.
I hope that this will help to answer some of your questions.

You should always remember that your mother tried very
hard for you all.

A note from the author

I HAVE JUST finished reading through the final edit of this book and would now like to make a few comments about Emma's illness.

I likened this whole period to the impending onslaught of a category five hurricane: the feeling that I was totally unable to control a situation; the knowledge of knowing this would be bad but not knowing how bad, or how furiously one was going to get thrown from pillar to post.

As this hurricane unleashed its destructive power upon our lives, instant answers were required on how to deal with people and situations, and I made decisions that could only be taken on the spur of the moment. Some of these decisions were very harsh and were made without the benefit of hindsight. I tried not to offend or cut anybody out during this almighty storm – and I apologise if anybody does feel offended. All I tried to do was manage its effects so that my children and I could rebuild our lives and I could get the four of us to where we are now: a place where the storm has passed, the sun is shining and we all can smile again.

As I say in this book, I was not the perfect husband or carer, nor was Emma the perfect patient during this time. But most of all I want this to be a truthful account of Emma's illness and its aftermath.

I think it is important that you, the reader, remember that this is only *my* account of an illness that is all too common and for which there are no hard and fast rules; that what I have said is only meant to help – strange as it may seem – those who have felt its effects in the past or are riding out their own storm at present. Things get said and actions taken that can make one feel guilty, alone and afraid; I want others to realise that these emotions are all totally normal, no matter how alien or unnatural they may feel.

Finally, I can feel the love I had, and still have, for Emma running through these pages and I hope that you do too.

Jon Nicholson
January 2008

Prologue

Going Neutrapenic and Other Medical Words

WE HAD BEEN WARNED it would happen. Emma and I both knew. We just didn't think it would happen quite so soon. 'Going neutrapenic': an expression that neither of us had ever heard of just two weeks before, but one we would become very familiar with very quickly. There is the old cliché that cancer is a word, not a sentence, which may be true for some. But cancer is also a whole new language, and anyone who comes into close contact with this illness is soon forced to learn it, and fast. I hadn't fully realised this until the events of that particular evening had finished unfolding at a speed that I was totally unprepared for. By the time I was finally able to catch my breath, I started to understand how little time I had to learn this language and adapt to the enormity of what had hit us as a family. I also saw that what lay ahead of us now would bear no relation to the life we had once led as a happy, settled, family of five.

On that particular day, Emma had been home for just two hours. I had done the three-hour round trip to collect her from the Middlesex Hospital, just off London's Tottenham Court Road, where she had spent the last four days as an in-patient on the Whitbread ward, one of the oncology wards. She had been diagnosed just over two weeks before, had just finished her first session of chemotherapy, and was determined to remain strong and positive throughout the months of treatment that stretched ahead. This was despite being told from the outset by the doctors that they were putting her on the strongest possible chemotherapy treatment, and that she had to know there was a chance the drugs would kill her, irrespective of what the cancer might do. Emma's reaction to this stark piece of information was quite simply, 'Just do whatever it takes to get rid of this thing.' This strong and beautiful woman was not going to get put off by any daunting-sounding treatment. As far as she was concerned, she would submit her body to anything, as long as it rid her of the osteosarcoma – the bone cancer – that was now eating away at her.

When I had collected her that afternoon, she looked fine and even sounded quite cheerful. She was sitting on her bed, waiting for me, her bag was packed, and she was ready to go home. We said goodbye to the nurses and to some of the patients that Emma, in her typical way, had already befriended. These were very temporary goodbyes: she was due back two days later for the start of her next round of chemo. But in the meantime, she was able to go home, see the children, cuddle them and make the most of some treasured time with them. She couldn't wait.

In the car on the way home, I thought she seemed surprisingly undamaged both physically and emotionally by what she had just been through. She had told me on the phone, when I'd spoken to her over the last few days, that sometimes she felt a bit sick, or her line, through which the drugs and the fluids were being pumped into her body, was a bit uncomfortable. But whatever she had gone through in hospital, she appeared to have coped with it well, and it didn't now seem to be affecting her. In fact, she was more interested in telling me about the lady in the bed opposite her who snored, so she hadn't managed to get much sleep, or that the food wasn't much good but that her friend Gina had brought in extra supplies in the form of Covent Garden soups, which had helped. I was secretly relieved: so far, so good.

When we eventually got back to Haslemere later that afternoon, we quickly collected the children from the friends down the road who had been looking after them, and arrived home, elated at the thought of the two entire days that lay ahead of us when we could be a family once again. Two days: the length of a weekend. Normally, we glide through weekends without thinking, knowing that the next one will be along soon enough. We look forward to them, of course, but we take them for granted. And because they come round with comforting regularity, they fly by and, before we know it, they're over and it's Sunday evening. But now, we were going to have to squeeze precious time as a family into two short days, knowing that Emma would soon be incapable of enjoying what passed for us as normal family life: going down to the beach with the children, windsurfing, having friends over for Sunday lunch. So this first time at home was a bonus: Emma seemed better than I had dared to expect, so I hoped our two days would provide us with some semblance of normality.

As soon as she got in through the front door, Emma went straight up to have a bath to get rid of the horrible hospital smell that always seems to linger on, long after you have left the ward. Soon, feeling cleansed and refreshed, she and the children were cuddling up on the sofa and catching up. They knew their mother had cancer because we had told them from the outset; they also knew that the treatment she was going to have, to try to make her better, would entail regular stays in hospital. Now that she was home after her first bout of treatment, they were understandably really happy to see their mum again, and started chatting away excitedly about what they had been doing during their final week of the summer holidays. Molly, who had just turned 10, was starting a new school in nearby Midhurst, so was giving Emma a full update on any new developments before the start of term, mainly involving speculation of who might be in which class, and how she really wanted to be in the same class as her best friends, and what a nightmare it would be if she wasn't. In other words, Molly was telling Emma about all the things which matter most to a normal, bubbly 10-year-old. Maisy, who was seven, and Sam, who was four and a half, were filling Emma in on their trip to the beach earlier that week, and what they had done that afternoon at their friends' house. The children didn't ask their mum many questions about what she had been up to in hospital, but they did notice that she had a small tube – a cannula – inserted into her hand, and heavy taping around it to keep it in place. As avid *Casualty* fans – or 'Cas', as we simply called it in our house, because it was such a Saturday evening fixture for Emma and the kids, who all loved it – this was like having a real-life episode in your front room. How great was that! So they were fascinated by this weird tube and what it was for.

Eventually, like all children, they wandered off to carry on with their day. Meanwhile, I was pottering around, doing some tidying up in the kitchen. Suddenly, I heard Emma calling out to me from the living room. I went in to see what was up.

Looking up from the sofa she was now lying on, she said to me rather flatly, 'I don't feel too good. Do you mind fixing the children's tea?'

'Riiight, well, that doesn't surprise me, given what you've been through,' I replied, hoping to sound matter-of-fact, although my initial thought had actually been, 'What, already? Jesus, this stuff is powerful shit if it's doing this to you this quickly!'

I duly went off, rustled something up for the children's tea, sat them down to eat it, then went back to check on Emma half an hour later. I walked into the front room and saw at once that she was shaking quite badly. We had been told that this might happen, so I knew that she needed to take her temperature: 99.7°F. Not great. I decided to call the chemotherapy nurse on the ward at the Middlesex, because even at that stage, I could tell this was a worrying sign. I got through straight away.

'Hi, this is Jon Nicholson, Emma's husband. She's not feeling too good right now, she's a bit red in the face.'

'OK. Has she got a temperature?'

'Yes, 99.7 degrees.'

'Oh . . . kay,' he answered slowly, in his lilting Scottish accent, as he thought carefully about the instructions he would issue next. 'I'd like you to take her temperature again in 10 minutes' time and ring me back.'

He was very calm. I waited for 10 minutes. The clock ticked slowly on . . . and on . . . and finally it was time to take Emma's temperature again. I almost didn't need to. I could see her visibly getting worse, before my very eyes. I took her temperature again and, in a mere 10 minutes, it had gone over the 100 mark. I dialled the direct line to the ward and spoke to the nurse again.

'Hello, Jon here. It's 100.4.'

'Okay, fine,' he replied, still calm. 'I think you should pack a bag, then take it again in 10 minutes' time and call me back.'

Another endless, endless wait for the minute hand on the clock to move on to the required time. Surely time was standing still, it couldn't go by *that* slowly, could it? Emma was getting worse by the minute and just lying there, shaking with fever. With the 10 minutes barely up, I took her temperature again and saw with mounting horror that it had jumped yet again. I quickly punched the numbers out for the ward, the now-familiar voice answered, and I got straight to the point.

'She's up to 102.6 degrees.'

'Okay, I think she's probably going to go neutrapenic,' the nurse replied, still admirably unflappable. 'Have you got someone there to look after the children? Call them now. Don't wait for an ambulance. Just take her to your nearest hospital. Now. Which one are you going to? The Royal Surrey in Guildford? Fine, I'll call A&E there, and they'll be ready and waiting for you when you get there.'

'But it will take us 20 minutes to get there.'

'Don't worry, that's fine, I'll let them know.'

I hung up and got straight on the phone to a friend of ours who lived nearby and who had offered to help out if ever we needed her. Now was that time.

'Kate, you need to come over now. I've got to take Emma to hospital immediately. She's not well . . .'

'Okay, Jon, I won't be long, but I'm right in the middle of my din—'

'No, Kate,' I interrupted, exasperated, 'you don't understand. I have to take Emma to the hospital – NOW.'

'Well, um, can you just give me 10 minutes to put my stuff together?'

'Kate, get over here, for fuck's sake!' I practically screamed down the phone at her, before slamming it down.

'Where's your stuff?' I asked Emma, who was now looking iller than I had ever seen her.

'Why?'

'Where's your stuff?'

Realising she was barely able to think straight, I rushed upstairs, threw the bare essentials into a small bag, and rushed back down to find the children in the front room, clearly very upset and scared, Molly in particular. They had finished their tea and had gone in to see their mother, only to find her lying there, clearly very unwell.

'It's okay, shush, don't worry kids, I'm just going to take Mummy to the hospital,' I said, as calmly as I could. 'Just go and sit over there, and don't make too much noise.'

'But what's wrong?' they cried.

They didn't understand: an hour ago, their mum had been chatting to them on that very sofa, apparently fine. Now she was almost incoherent with fever. As the children clung to her, in tears, she tried to give them a hug and to reassure them: 'I don't know what's wrong, but don't worry, I'll be back shortly.' I got Emma up, wrapping my arms around her to prevent her from falling, and as she stumbled out of the house, she was still trying to smile at her children as she mumbled, 'It's okay, I'll be back soon.'

I didn't have time to feel scared, or to panic. I didn't have time to feel my guts twisting inside me at the sight of my sobbing, frightened children. I just knew this was a very serious situation and it had to be sorted out as quickly as possible.

I got Emma to the car just as Kate's daughter pulled up. She had obviously managed to rush out more quickly than her mother. There was no time for niceties. But I do remember making a mental note that we clearly weren't going to be able to rely on Kate – or not in this way, at least – if, every time I called, she wasn't able to drop everything, and come straight over. The way I saw it, ever since I had heard Emma's diagnosis, I had made it my priority to do everything I could to enable her and the children to get through the horror of what lay ahead, and I needed to know who I could truly count on to help me to do this. I realise that people who have not been in my situation might think I was being harsh towards Kate, but all I could think about at this stage – because I knew there was a possibility that Emma might actually die that evening – was battening down the hatches and protecting, as best I could, those I loved the most. And if, in so doing, I came across as impatient with some people, then that did not overly concern me. I didn't let on to Kate that I had decided she was not going to be of much help in an emergency, but equally, I wasn't going to worry about offending her at that moment. I simply didn't have time. I poured Emma into the car, ran back in to get the overnight bag, then set off for the hospital as fast as safety would allow me. All the way there, I kept wondering how much higher Emma's temperature now was, and how much higher it could go before it would kill her?

Chemotherapy kills bad cells, but also a lot of good cells. And amongst the good cells it kills are the white cells in our blood. These are essential for fighting off infection, and if their levels drop too low, our bodies become unable to resist all the bacteria that we naturally carry inside us. This causes a fever and, eventually, if left untreated, septicaemia sets in when the infection takes over. Our immune system collapses, our vital organs cease to function, and we die. Emma had neutrapenic fever, and it is a common side-effect of chemotherapy and one which they warn you about. What I think hadn't been made fully clear – or maybe it was just one of those details that we hadn't fully taken on board, amongst the thousands of other details, when the treatment had been explained to us – was that this could happen even after the first bout of treatment. And also that it could happen that fast and that violently. That was why we had been taken by surprise. Emma was to go neutrapenic on several more occasions during the course of her chemotherapy, but it was never as frightening as that first time.

On the way to the hospital, I could see that Emma was terrified. She didn't know what was going to happen. Every minute that went by, she was getting worse. Finally, after what seemed like an interminable journey, we pulled up outside A&E. I left Emma in the car, ran in and went straight up to the nurse on triage duty, 'Bed! Now! Neutrapenic!', as I pointed frantically in the general direction of my car that was parked right outside the entrance. All credit to the Middlesex, they had rung on ahead of us, as they had promised, and warned the Royal Surrey that Emma was coming in, so I had hardly had time to say those words before staff were wheeling a trolley out to the car and getting Emma on to it. She was taken straight to a side room in A&E. No need or time for paperwork at this stage. Everyone was rushing around her like blue-arsed flies. A doctor appeared from nowhere, an antibiotic drip was immediately set up and pumped straight into her arm (thank God the cannula was already in place!) and a nurse was assigned to care for her. When there is an emergency, I truly believe the NHS is there for you. They certainly were this time, and it didn't matter at all that the nurse could hardly speak English: she knew exactly what she was doing and was fantastically efficient. And that, in the end, was all that mattered.

Finally, Emma's condition was stabilised. Just in time. 'This is going to be unbelievable,' I stood there thinking, as I looked down at my semi-conscious wife, and took stock of what had happened in the space of just a couple of hours. 'This is what it's going to be like, now. And I'd better be prepared for it.'

By the time Emma was out of danger and it was safe for me to leave the hospital, it was almost midnight. I arrived home to find Molly waiting up and wanting answers to questions. Sam and Maisy had gone to bed, finally overcome by exhaustion, but I owed it to Molly to explain to her what was going on, and to allay any fears she might have had. Maybe because she was older than the others, she had been particularly upset by the scene that had unfolded before her eyes so quickly and dramatically earlier that evening, and the sight of her mother shaking uncontrollably with fever had clearly affected her. So it was vital – as it always was before and has been since – that I reassure her and tell her why it had happened. By the time I had finished, Molly was able to go to bed safe, in the knowledge that, once the doctors made her better, her mum would indeed be coming home.

I eventually collapsed into bed, my head buzzing with the events of the day, my body crying out for rest. I had managed to cope with this hurdle, but I knew that I would be jumping many, many more. This was no ordinary obstacle course, because with Emma's illness, I never knew how soon the next hurdle would come, nor how high it would be – nor indeed whether I would manage to clear it.

The next day dawned, and the first challenge was to talk to Maisy and Sam, who had gone to sleep without knowing what had happened to their mother. And who, no sooner had their mother come home, had seen her snatched away from them. When would they next be seeing her? As with Molly, I had to make the time to sit down and explain to them what I knew and what was going on. I had to answer their questions in a language which a little boy of four and a half and a slightly older girl of seven could understand. And if they didn't understand first time round, I had to find another way of giving them the information they were asking for. It took time, thought and honesty to do that. And I made it my absolute priority to make sure I communicated with all my children in such a way that they felt utterly able to ask me about anything, at any time. To my mind, that was the only way in which they would cope with the awfulness of what I knew they would have to face in the months and years to come.

Once I had finished talking to the children, I got on the phone to the hospital to see how Emma had been through the night. The news was good. Being young and fit, her body had reacted well to the antibiotics that were now flooding her system. The doctors were optimistic and hoped she would be able to go home in a day or two. The trouble was, she was due back the following day at the Middlesex for her next four-day chemotherapy session, and I knew Emma would have been devastated if she had had to postpone it. As it turned out, she was discharged from hospital the very next morning, just 36 hours after being admitted in such a critical condition that death could have been hours away.

The joy the children had in seeing their mother walk back into the house was short-lived, because they had to be told that later that morning she would have to leave again and go back to the hospital in London. Yet again, their mother was being taken away from them before they had barely had a chance to hold her in their arms. Not only was I having to learn to cope with daily hurdles, not only was Emma having to cope with her illness and all its terrible consequences, but the children were also having to learn that, for the time being at least, this is what their life was going to be: a constant emotional assault course.

I

Early Days

By the time I met Emma in 1989, I was 28 years old and had managed to carve out for myself a reasonably good career as a photographer. I specialised in windsurfing photography and spent a lot of time abroad on shoots for magazines or equipment manufacturers, but I also did more general magazine and editorial work. However, my route to photography had been anything but straightforward, as indeed had been my route in life.

I was adopted when I was two days old. My adoptive parents were childless at that stage, and my father was a highly successful anaesthetist whose team was instrumental in developing the epidural anaesthesia that has so revolutionised childbirth for women. My mother was a nurse but she had stopped work when I came along. My parents then adopted a little girl when I was two but, rather surprisingly, went on to have their own natural child, a girl, when I was 10 years old.

Although we lived a very cosy life in Dulwich, by the age of 11, I had a difficult relationship with my parents and was often in conflict with them. Whereas my younger sister was the perfect pupil, I struggled at school, however hard I tried. In the end, I was sent away at the age of 12 to a horrible boarding school,

Cliff View House – no doubt, and hopefully, long since closed down – in Seaford, Sussex. Why was I sent away? Because I had been diagnosed as dyslexic and my parents were desperate for me to pass the Common Entrance exam at the age of 13 in order to get into a 'decent' secondary boarding school, and Cliff View House specialised in teaching what were then seen as academic no-hopers such as me. There were only five or six children per class and the teachers literally crammed us, in the hope that somehow we might just slip under the net and get accepted somewhere at 13. The regime was so intense that we only went home to see our parents one weekend a term, unlike normal boarding schools where there are three or four exeat weekends per term. Other than an all-pervasive feeling of loneliness, my only specific memory of my time at Cliff View House was sitting on Brighton beach one day with my parents, sobbing, and just wanting to know why they'd sent me to this school.

By this stage, I think I had subconsciously decided that if that was what they wanted for me, that was fine, but I no longer wanted to spend time at home either. I didn't fit in, as far as I could see, I didn't live up to their hopes and aspirations, my relationship with my mother in particular was deteriorating by the week, and the one with my father was, at best, distant.

Despite my best efforts, I still failed the Common Entrance exam. Fortunately, I somehow got accepted into a minor public school called Bearwood College, near Wokingham, largely on the basis that I was, firstly, good at sport, cricket in particular, secondly, good at art, and thirdly, a jolly decent sort – all of primary importance in the English public school system. So amazingly, and much to my relief, I went off there and had a pretty good time. I played a lot of cricket, did well at it, and ignored the fact that, academically, I was a disaster, thanks to my dyslexia. But one of the best things to come out of my time at Bearwood College was the fact that I met Paul, who soon became my closest friend.

Paul's parents ran very successful businesses and lived in Chelsea, just opposite the Chelsea Arts Club. Before long, I was spending every exeat weekend and most of the holidays with them, although, in reality, Paul and I practically lived at the Arts Club. His family were – and are – lovely, and they made me feel so welcome that, even when Paul stayed on at school after O levels, I was still able to stay with them whenever I wanted to.

It would have been out of the question for me to contemplate the idea of doing A levels, but when my O level results did come through, even I could not have anticipated my father's response. Holding up the piece of paper on which it was written that I had passed one solitary O level, a B in Art, he just stood in the hall of our house, looked at me and, with a sigh, uttered the words which haunt me still, 'Couldn't you at least have tried a bit harder,' before walking past, his lips pursed in disappointment.

Shortly before leaving school a couple of months earlier, I had had the 'Well, what are you going to do with yourself?' conversation with my parents. 'We can't have you hanging around the house doing nothing,' they had added supportively. So it was decided that I should apply to one of the management trainee schemes run by the John Lewis Partnership. Despite my apparent lack of qualifications, I managed to get accepted and, to my surprise, had the time of my life. I found I was actually quite good at the job, there were lots of pretty girls working there, and I soon got to know all there was to know about the fourth-floor stock room of the garden furniture section of Peter Jones, Sloane Square!

I was only 17 and having a blast. I had a job I liked, was earning a bit of money, was partying hard, and had total independence from my parents, whom I saw only rarely. One July morning, though, I came home from a party in the early hours, rather the worse for wear, only to find my father sitting on the stairs in his pyjamas, waiting up for me. He had never done this before. 'For once, you could have come home a bit earlier. I needed to talk to you.'

I looked at him in disbelief. 'Well, if you'd wanted to talk to me, why didn't you do that before I went out?' I replied as I clambered past him on my way up to my room.

I just wasn't prepared to have a discussion with him at four in the morning, after God knows how many pints of Newcastle Ale and some Liebfraumilch to top things off. The next morning, I was woken up by some noise and commotion downstairs. By the time I got down there, my mother was standing alone in the kitchen, looking awkward and flustered. She told me that my father had gone into hospital early that morning; he had leukaemia and he had not long to live.

It took a few moments for the news to sink in. I was completely shocked and appalled. How could I start to comprehend the enormity of what I had just heard? I was furious with both my parents for not telling me. I was even angrier when I found out that, in fact, he had been ill for seven years. Seven years! How could they have kept this from me for all that time? In doing so, I felt they had treated me as if I didn't matter, as if it wasn't necessary for me to know, as if I was a piece of shit. I felt totally and utterly let down by them. Or rather, let down by them a second time. The first had been when they had packed me off to boarding school, where I was desperately unhappy, because as far as I was concerned they couldn't accept me for who I was, because they couldn't accept that I wasn't going to be what they had planned.

Barely one month after I was told the truth about my father's illness, he died. Having hidden it from me for all that time, ironically, my mother made me go and see him lying on his deathbed in hospital, even though it was the last thing I had felt like doing.

~

Soon after my father's death, my mother made it pretty clear that she expected me to move out. She had met the man whom she would go on to marry, Neil, who is a vicar, and she told me that she needed to get on with her life. If I had ever had any doubts in the past that I did not belong at home, those doubts had now become a certainty.

After four more years at Peter Jones, I went to work for Nashua, a company that supplied office equipment. Aged 22, I was sharing a flat in Battersea with Paul, I was a successful salesman, and I was earning a lot of money. I then got promoted into their marketing department. Nashua sponsored a couple of powerboats and before long, as part of my job, I started to travel around Europe, photographing these boats during races. This was great fun and I loved the life of a photographer so much that eventually I had to make a decision: either I carried on working for Nashua, or I took up photography full-time. I chose the latter.

I had made friends along the way with a guy called Mark Woods, or 'Woodsy', who was a professional windsurfer. I had taken up the sport myself some years back and had quickly developed a passion for it. So I started travelling with him to the Canary Islands or to Hawaii, where he did a lot of surfing, and I earned a bit of money selling photographs to windsurfing magazines, or doing photos for sail or board manufacturers. In 1987, I spent the best part of the year in Los Angeles, partly because it was a convenient place to get to Hawaii from, and partly because I was doing freelance work for Allsport, the enormously successful British sports photography agency. My goal by then was to join them as a staffer, so when the opportunity arose to do so back in London, I packed my bags and returned to the UK. In order to rise up the ranks at Allsport, I had to be prepared to start on the lowest rung of the ladder, and if that meant doing the wet Tuesday night in December on the touchline at White Hart Lane, then that's what I had to do. And I did. I stuck at it, because I so wanted to be part of the Allsport set-up. In hindsight, I was never a football photographer, nor a hard action photographer. I think that sort of sports photography is difficult and you have to want to do it. My sort of sports photography was not in that style, and I eventually recognised that working for Allsport would not be a long-term professional route for me. I was just gaining this realisation when I met Emma.

Emma was 21 and worked at the Chelsea Arts Club. Founded originally by the artist John Whistler, it's a place for artists, writers, actors and such like to meet, have a beer, play snooker, have a meal, talk and have a bed for the night if they need one. It's more bohemian than the traditional gentleman's club and, certainly in the past, was probably a den of iniquity. The bar area where the snooker tables are looks out on to a beautiful shady garden, and the office where Emma worked was near the front door and between the bar and the stairs that led upstairs to the bedrooms.

I used to have this running joke with Woodsy, as we travelled around, that I'd see some woman or other, and I'd go, 'God, I could marry a girl like that!' and he'd reply, 'Oh shut up, Jon! And get me another beer while you're at it.' It didn't take me long, though, to notice that Emma was absolutely gorgeous, that I definitely wanted to ask her out, and that although I hadn't actually spoken to her yet, I was going to marry her. When I told Mark this, he just laughed at the tired old joke. 'No, seriously, Woodsy, I *am* going to marry that girl!'

Emma was beautiful. Simple as that. She was slim, not too tall, with the most incredible mane of curly light chestnut hair, and piercing grey eyes. She was always smiling at me, and, for me at least, it really was love at first sight. But, somehow, I just couldn't seem to pluck up the courage to ask her out. I would notice her flitting from the office to the bar, giving people messages, greeting people. I'd manage to exchange a few words with her when I would find a plausible excuse for dropping by the office. But she was never alone there, so in order to actually ask her on a date, I had to resort to extreme measures: I went up to the first floor of the club, where there was a payphone, and called her up from there. How desperate was that? But the gods were smiling on me that day, because luckily she agreed to come out to dinner with me later that week.

We went to a restaurant round the back of Camden market, and I was really terrified I would mess it up. I had travelled around quite a bit by then, and had had a fair number of casual relationships, but I had not actually dated many women, so I was very nervous. We had a nice evening, and she agreed to come out with me again on what turned out to be Boxing Day. This time, we went on a double date with Woodsy and his then girlfriend, a rather lively Swedish girl. 'I'll come and pick you up from your parents, then we'll go up to London for dinner.' This was only date number two, but already Emma was happy to introduce me to her parents, her three older brothers and her grandmother, all of whom had gathered at her house for Christmas. I took this to be a good sign. Other than the fact that, in those days, nothing much was open on Boxing Day evening and we ended up in a pub somewhere in north London, the evening was a success and Emma stayed over.

The next day, Woodsy and I were off to the Canary Islands for three weeks of windsurfing and photography, so I left Emma behind in London with a heavy heart. By then, though, I was totally loved up! After a brief period back in England, I had to go off for a further two weeks on a work assignment to the Caribbean with another friend of mine, Pete Hart. This time, the lovesickness kicked in hard. At every opportunity, I would call her: 'Hi, miss you,' 'Only another 10 days,' 'Can't wait to be with you.' The usual nonsense that two people say to each other when they have just embarked on a passionate relationship. I was on the phone every spare second. I was a complete bore, always nipping off, and saying to Pete, 'I'm just going to ring Emma.' So much so that he joked I could have saved myself money by *flying* her out to where we were, because that would surely have cost less than my phone bill.

On my return, our relationship developed quickly. I felt I had truly found someone I could share my life with, and when Emma got pregnant unexpectedly, six months later, I knew I wanted to keep the baby and start a family with her. Emma was thrilled that I shared her desire to have the baby, and we could not have been happier. Then, three months into the pregnancy, and for no apparent reason, she suffered a miscarriage. This was devastating for us both, but particularly for Emma, and it left her feeling vulnerable and afraid regarding my commitment to the relationship. Now that we were no longer going to have a baby this was, after all, my opportunity to opt out, and to walk away from a long-term relationship with her. For me, though, there was never any question: I had found Emma, and was not going to let her go, whatever happened. And a few months later, less than a year after meeting her, I asked her to marry me.

On 1 June 1991, we got married. It was a very traditional English church wedding, in Hersham, Surrey, near where her parents lived and where Emma had grown up. Emma looked dazzlingly beautiful and I was a blissfully happy man. After the ceremony, we went up to London for the reception, which was held in the impeccably groomed grounds of the Hurlingham Club, in Fulham, before flying off to the Dominican Republic for our honeymoon. We spent two weeks in a little beachside hotel, paid for by Woodsy; I spent most afternoons surfing, while Emma would lie sunning herself, looking as if she had just taken a break from a fashion shoot.

For the first couple of years after we got married, Emma continued working at the Arts Club, whilst I, having left Allsport, started getting more sports and feature work for the newspapers. At the start of 1993, Emma got pregnant again, which was fantastic, and, soon after, I started covering Damon Hill's Formula 1 career, now that he had joined the Williams team. Damon was a close friend of mine, whom I had met 10 years earlier when he was working as a lowly motorcycle courier boy. We had shared a good number of raucous nights out, and, despite his now elevated status as the new hope of British Formula 1, he hadn't changed as a person and had kept many of his old friends. It also helped that Emma got on very well with his wife, Georgie.

The idea behind following Damon's first year as a Williams driver was to provide coverage for him in the papers and raise his profile, thanks to the access I already had to them. He had started to do some behind-the-scenes and 'at-home' interviews, and he wanted someone he could trust to do the photographs. The partnership worked so well that, the following year, 1994, when Damon got the number 1 drive, following Alain Prost's departure, we decided to do a book – part text, part photographs – showing what life was like for him not only during the races but behind the scenes at the circuits as well. The book was a big success, probably all the more so because Damon also talked about what it had been like to race in the same team as the iconic Ayrton Senna, who had been killed that year in a brutal accident during the San Marino Grand Prix at Imola. In any event, doing the book opened up a whole new career change for me and meant that, for the next two years, I would continue to cover motor racing and Damon's career for nine months of the year. Although motor racing was not actually a sport I was attracted to, and the novelty regarding the supposed glamour of it all soon wore off, I was pleased to have got such lucrative work.

Meanwhile, Emma's pregnancy had not been great: she had developed complications, including fluid in the womb, which meant that the baby was very small. She then developed pre-eclampsia which, if left untreated, is potentially fatal for mother and baby, so five weeks before term, the doctors had to perform an emergency Caesarean. Molly was born safely, thankfully, but weighed only three pounds, half what she should normally have weighed at that stage. She went straight to the Special Care Unit at St Thomas' hospital, where Emma had chosen to have the baby, and spent the next three weeks gaining strength and weight. Molly is now a strong and healthy girl, but her start in life was certainly a bit shaky and premature.

Soon after Molly was born, we left Clapham, where we had been living in a small one-bedroom flat, and, with the money we got from selling that, bought a comfortable, three-bedroom townhouse in Haslemere, Surrey, with a long, mature garden. It was perfect: near enough to the station and to the trains back to London, which was essential for my work, but also near enough to the beaches where we could take the baby and go surfing. We already had a few friends who lived in the area – Damon being one of them – and Emma soon made many more. Haslemere provided us with a completely different quality of life and before long we were fully settled in to our new surroundings and were planning more children.

Unfortunately, it took a bit longer than we had anticipated, because Emma miscarried the next two pregnancies, each time at the three-month mark, and just when we thought we were in the clear. Each time, Emma was distraught, because all she ever wanted to be in life was a mother. Her mother and grandmother had both had children in their early twenties, and Emma wanted to do the same. As far as she was concerned, that is what she had been put on this planet to do. She already adored being a mother to Molly and she couldn't wait to have more children and to devote her life to them. Eventually, in June 1996, our second little girl was born. As with Molly, the birth was anything but straightforward. This time, the baby was late, the cord got wrapped around her neck, the heartbeat started to slow down, so Emma had another emergency Caesarean. In the end, everything was fine and Maisy was healthy and perfect. By the time Emma became pregnant again, three years later, it was not a question of when she might give birth, it was very much 'You *will* be having your baby on this date, by elective Caesarean'. So our little boy, Sam, was born, as planned, on 4 March 1999. He was a wonderful addition to our family that we now felt was complete.

By then, I had stopped doing Formula 1 and was working on more specific photographic projects, often instigated by me. Although these involved me going away for periods of time, I was also at home a lot and able to share the task of bringing up our children. My relationship with Emma was still very loving and, although we bickered and got annoyed with each other like any normal couple, there weren't any major tensions or long-term problems between us. I had never felt the need to look at any other woman, because Emma gave me everything I needed. She really was my best friend and my closest confidante. For the first time, I felt I could tell someone everything that was on my mind, I could share with her any worries I had, I could bounce ideas off her regarding my work. It didn't matter what I said, she was always supportive, always positive. Yes, she sometimes worried about money, and about when I would next get work. But she never let that stop me pursuing my career and doing what I felt I needed to do. And despite having three small children to care for, which is inevitably tiring and all-consuming, we still managed to laugh a lot and to enjoy ourselves; we hadn't lost sight of what had drawn us together in the first place.

We had created a solid family unit and, at that stage, life was serene and secure. Emma was incredible with the children and would blow everyone away: for example, she would push the boat out at all their birthday parties, would remember everyone else's birthdays, and would get them presents that showed she had thought about what they would like to receive. She was the sort of person who, when it came to finding a light for the birthday cake candles, would have anticipated the moment and would produce the matches right on cue.

As far as our wider family was concerned, Emma was very close to her mother, saw her regularly, and would often visit her parents with the children, particularly when I was away on my trips abroad. In contrast, I had very little contact with my two sisters, whose lives were very different from mine. My younger sister, after gaining a degree from Cambridge, was now a doctor, whilst I had never been remotely close to my youngest sister who was 10 years younger than me and who, to all intents and purposes, had never lived under the same roof as me for more than a few weeks at a time. I continued to maintain a clear distance between me and my mother. Our relationship was still based on conflict and I saw no point in pretending we got on. It was to Emma's enormous credit that, when the children were born, she insisted on regularly taking the children over to see my mother so that they could develop a relationship with her. I knew that mine with her would never be good, so had long ago decided to be emotionally self-sufficient when it came to my family. Indeed, as far as I was concerned, my family was not the one I had grown up with, but the one I now had with Emma. They were my emotional refuge, and that is where I felt loved, and could love. And that would always be the case.

2

The Skies Begin
To Darken

LOOKING BACK, I suppose the yogurts were the first clue. Emma never normally got ill; she barely even got colds. Like most mothers with young children, she never allowed herself to fall ill, so on the rare occasions when she did feel unwell, she would simply battle through. During 2002, however, Emma started to feel tired and run down in a way that she never had up until then. She also developed regular colds and had a permanently stuffy nose.

She assumed, as did I, that she was simply paying the price for having three children under the age of seven, and for wanting to be the dedicated, ever-present mother to them. That autumn, she picked up a cold that she was simply unable to shake off. She tried every homeopathic remedy available, because we had treated other minor ailments successfully using this method, but still the cold persisted, as well as the blocked nose. I remember her walking around during that time with a constant sniffle and a tissue permanently lodged in the palm of her hand. Eventually, she went to the doctor who told her that it could be down to the area having a lot of mosses: they could be causing some sort of allergic reaction in the lining of her sinuses. And, he added, it was not surprising she was regularly tired and under the weather: having three young children was physically demanding, however enjoyable it also was, and it was common for mothers to pick up a lot of bugs when their children were young and mixing with other bug-infested children. So all in all, not to worry. It would sort itself out in due course. So Emma didn't worry, and just carried on as usual.

Throughout our married life, if I hadn't done something she'd asked me to do, or if I had done it wrong – for example, if I hadn't taken a box of stuff up to the attic that she'd asked me to take, and she had ended up doing it herself – Emma had had this strange habit of saying to me, 'What if I die? You'd have to do it yourself,' or 'What if I die? I don't know how you'd manage.' I know many women – and particularly busy mothers – have a tendency to say these things, or at least to think them. But because Emma was not a pessimist or a hypochondriac in any way, it would always come as a surprise to hear her say it, and it also sounded uncharacteristically dramatic. So I would never take any notice. I would usually just apologise for not having done what I was supposed to, and tried to get out of the doghouse by making myself useful in some other way.

One afternoon in September of 2002, when Emma was starting to suffer from her permanent cold, she asked me if I could go down to the supermarket and do a shop. No problem. I was used to doing that, using the shopping list on the back of the fridge door that we updated as we ran out of things. 'And don't forget to get stuff for the packed lunches,' she called after me, as I went out the door. I didn't need reminding what those comprised of, so I knew that I had to get ham, bread, Babybel cheese, yogurts and fruit.

An hour or so later, I was back and Emma was helping me to unpack the carrier bags in the kitchen when she suddenly looked up and, in a total fury, shouted, 'You've forgotten the yogurts!' God, how could I have been so forgetful? They were on my mental list, but somehow I'd managed to come home without them. Before I had time to apologise or to explain that I'd just go back tomorrow and get some, she screamed, 'If I die of cancer, how are you going to cope?'

I wasn't shocked by the fact that she was screaming – it wasn't the first time she had done it. And I wasn't shocked by the fact that she'd said 'if I die'. She'd said that before, too. What did stun me was the fact that she'd added the really absurd variation 'if I die of cancer'. Why the fuck did she say that, I thought. It was so outlandish and so precise, as if her dying from that particular illness meant I wouldn't cope, whereas if she'd died from something else I would have done. Why didn't she just say, 'If I go under a bus,' or 'If I die in an accident'? No. 'If I die of cancer.' I was left totally speechless. In fact, if I had said anything at that stage, she would probably have gone on a complete rant. So I said nothing, turned away, and carried on silently unpacking the bags. I thought no more about it, and just parked it somewhere deep in my subconscious as just a really weird thing to have said.

What I didn't know, and didn't find out until after her death, was that Emma had been having pain in her left knee for much of that year but because it wasn't unbearable, she hadn't told me, and had just soldiered on, as she always did when she wasn't feeling 100 per cent. She had mentioned it, though, to a friend of ours whose own knees are permanently bad. One day, over the summer, she had asked him in passing how his knees were. 'Not too good, at the moment,' and she had replied,

'Actually, my knee's been killing me too.' But when this friend recounted the conversation to me, he emphasised that she had made the comment in a casual 'something to talk about' way, in much the same way that two tennis players will compare notes about their respective tennis elbows or creaky hips. There was no element of worry in her manner or in her tone, and he forgot about it until many months later.

It is possible, though, that subconsciously Emma was starting to feel that all was not right. Certainly, in retrospect, I can see that her body's immune system was starting to fall apart and the first signs of her illness were beginning to manifest themselves. But at that stage, neither of us had any idea that her minor ailments could have been hiding something catastrophic.

The first visible sign that anything was wrong came at the start of February 2003. The south of England had just been crippled – as is always the way – by a few inches of snow which had fallen suddenly and very thickly, though not unexpectedly. People had been stranded overnight in their cars on motorways, all trains had come to a standstill and children, to their great excitement, had had the day off school. I have photographs of our children frolicking on a nearby expanse of fresh, virgin snow and sledging down the slope, totally exhilarated, as if they were body surfing in the ocean. Emma looks beautiful in those photographs, the hood of her jacket up to keep her warm in the chilly air; but she also appears absent. When I look at those photographs now, all I can see is the bags under her eyes and how tired and empty she looks.

A couple of days later, with our garden now slippery from the melted snow, she set off to retrieve the washing from the tumble dryer which, due to lack of space in the kitchen, was housed in the garden shed. Our garden was on quite a steep slope and was terraced. On the lowest level was the patio just outside the back of the house. Steps led up to the main part of the garden which then sloped upwards in a series of different levels, and the shed was about two-thirds of the way along the lawn. As Emma walked back down towards the house, carrying a full basket of laundry, she slipped and twisted her knee. Or rather, her knee twisted as it buckled under her. 'God, I've just slipped over and twisted my knee,' she announced matter-of-factly as she walked back into the kitchen. As she didn't seem to be in any undue pain, I don't remember what my response was. Certainly, the way she had told me didn't warrant any special comment. It certainly wasn't a question of me leaping over to grab the washing off her and saying, 'Take it easy, go and sit down.' Given the slope of the garden, I myself had slipped and fallen over on several occasions, in summer as well as winter. It was just one of those things you had to be a bit careful about, especially if you were carrying something at the time. Emma didn't mention it again and, other than hobbling around a bit for the rest of the day, the episode was forgotten about. It definitely didn't merit a visit to the doctor at that stage, we thought.

After a few weeks, the pain she felt from her fall must have still been there, as Emma did eventually go off to the doctor. She didn't tell me she was going, because I'm sure she assumed the problem was minor. The GP, who is a lovely man and part of a wonderful little country practice, listened to her describing her symptoms and arranged for her to have some physio at our local hospital in Haslemere, as he thought Emma had done some ligament damage. It was on her return from the GP that Emma informed me that she would soon be having weekly physio because that knee problem she had had the previous month hadn't gone away. This was all news to me, because she hadn't been limping or complaining of any pain, and her knee was not preventing her from leading a perfectly normal life. As I had had ligament and cartilage problems in various limbs that in the past had required surgery and physiotherapy, I was not remotely concerned.

And so it was that, once a week, from March until June, Emma diligently went for hour-long physiotherapy sessions with a cheerful young Aussie girl who did everything she could to get rid of this recalcitrant injury. Some nights, Emma was forced to lie with a pillow between her legs because she said the physiotherapy was making her knee really sore but presumably this was a good sign. In any event, the next day the severe pain had usually subsided. It might reappear later that evening, but Emma would take the view that she'd obviously overdone it that day. Similarly, her knee sometimes swelled up, and some days the swelling was actually pretty substantial. But on other days the knee would be back to normal. Swelling is caused by fluid which is there to protect the joint when it has been damaged, so again, we would link the swelling back to the fact that the knee had been under too much strain.

Emma never complained about the pain, and she never took any painkillers for it. Nor did we talk about it every day. Sometimes she would ask me to go to the shops for her because her knee was a bit sore, but I wasn't questioning her on a daily basis on the progress or otherwise of her injury. I never thought her symptoms were anything other than classic ligament or cartilage damage, and I assumed they would go away in due course.

Once, during this time, Emma did show some concern and said, 'God, what if it's cancer?' On that occasion, I remember being quite sharp with her. 'Look, if you think it's cancer, go back to the doctor and get it checked out. Tomorrow. Get on to it. Because if it is and you leave it . . .' I said this out of frustration, not because I seriously thought she had a tumour. But if she was really worried about it, she should just go and do something about it.

In the end, the decision was taken out of her hands. The physiotherapist turned round to her soon after and said, 'I think you should get this checked out because I'm not making any headway.' Which was hardly surprising, given what was really going on inside that knee joint. I think the physio's words scared Emma a bit because she did go back to the GP who arranged for her to have an X-ray in the next few days at the Royal Surrey County Hospital in Guildford and afterwards to see a consultant orthopaedic surgeon, Mark Flannery, who worked not only at the Royal Surrey but also at Haslemere Hospital. My initial thought, when Emma told me she was being sent for an X-ray, was, 'Damn, she'll probably have to have an operation on her knee and she'll be out of action for a few weeks or even months.' But that was the extent of my concerns, which were borne out of frustration, rather than real worry. It never occurred to me that the problem was anything remotely catastrophic.

I was away working when she had the X-ray and although I nipped home for a few days just after, I was away again when she saw Mr Flannery to have the results. I had renewed my association with Formula 1 that year, not through my own desire to plunge back into motor racing, but because Olympus, who were still supplying me with equipment, had themselves linked up to supply highly technical optical equipment for Ferrari. In return, I was to be given total access to the Ferrari team and staff and was to produce photographs that would then be shown all over the world. For everyone concerned, it was a good deal. And for me, financially, it was great, as I was being paid handsomely to do this work. The trouble was that the Grand Prix season began in March and ended at the end of October, which meant I would be away an enormous amount during those eight months. The races themselves were usually every other weekend, but sometimes the schedule was such that they were held on successive weekends. For example, that was the case for the British Grand Prix at Silverstone and the German Grand Prix in Hockenheim, which were held on back-to-back weekends that year. Even when the races were every two weeks, in between times there were separate photo shoots at the Ferrari headquarters in Maranello, near Bologna, and at other places around Europe. These took place either when the cars were being tested, or when special days were set aside for the various sponsors. In any event, taking on this work was a big commitment, but, after 15 years of association with Olympus, I was not going to jeopardise my relationship with them by being difficult and not turning up to a race 'just because' my wife was going for an X-ray and a doctor's appointment. I was my family's sole breadwinner, I had to support them financially, so I had no choice but to keep attending the races and whichever shoots I was also required for during the season.

So Emma went off to see Mark Flannery on her own. When she called me with the results, I was actually weaving my way down the Italian motorway on my way to Bologna to catch a plane the following morning after doing a full day's photo shoot for Ferrari. In the car with me was Sara, who was the marketing director at Olympus and was in charge of the Ferrari sponsorship. I had known Sara for a few years, and considered her a friend of mine, so the planned stop-over in a hotel between Bologna and Imola would be a very pleasant way of cooling down after a long and exhausting day on the tarmac at Maranello, photographing these extraordinary, noisy machines under the searingly hot July sun. I answered the phone and Emma told me that the consultant was very nice, but he had said that they couldn't see too much what was going on from the X-ray, so he was sending her back to Guildford to have an MRI scan. 'What do you think that means?' she asked me, with the first detectable trace of anxiety in her voice.

I was taken aback by what she was telling me, but I tried to make the right noises and to sound completely calm over the phone. If I sounded scared or worried, then Emma would notice and get worried herself. As it was, she was probably already terrified at that point; she just wasn't showing it. 'Don't worry, I'll be back tomorrow,' I tried to reassure her, 'we'll talk about it then.' I hung up, and just shouted at the top of my voice 'Shit, shit, shit!' This had suddenly moved on from me thinking 'Oh damn, this is going to be inconvenient for a few weeks' to 'This is fucking serious shit. This is going to get a whole lot worse than a bit of cartilage or ligament damage. We don't know what it is, but whatever it is, it has the potential for being pretty nasty.'

That evening, sipping a glass of champagne with Sara on the terrace of this beautiful old hotel nestled in the rolling Italian hills,

I looked out at the dream-like view and thought that there was nothing idyllic about being here. All I could think about was getting home. I didn't want to be stuck here, putting up a front, forced to spin out the evening with someone who I didn't want to be with, however much I liked them. I felt totally frustrated and helpless.

I now know that the X-ray report Mr Flannery read from the radiographer at the Royal Surrey didn't really say, 'We can't see what's going on here. Suggest you send the patient for a scan.' What was more likely was that it indicated grave concern at what was already visible, but that further scans and tests were needed in order to determine exactly what the problem was – and indeed its extent. Would the radiographer have mentioned the word 'tumour' or 'suspected tumour' at this stage? Yes, absolutely. But, like all good doctors, Mr Flannery was not going to reveal anything until he knew exactly what he could say. So when he saw Emma, he did not cause panic in her by hazarding a diagnosis. And also, fortunately, she didn't ask questions that he might have found awkward to answer at this stage.

As he realised that this was no ordinary problem, he made sure that an appointment was made immediately. Yet again, the NHS were there when we needed them, because there was no need to wait for referral letters, or for appointments that were weeks or months ahead. The doctor saw that this was urgent, and Emma got seen within a week.

I got home from Italy and Emma seemed surprisingly relaxed about the scan. In fact, she didn't bring it up, other than to say it had been scheduled for the following week, and that Flannery was, as luck would have it, free to see her the following day to explain the results. However, as bad luck would have it, I was away for most of that week at the German Grand Prix, in Hockenheim, so I would not be able to accompany Emma either to the scan, nor to the subsequent appointment with Mr Flannery, which actually fell on her 35th birthday. None of this appeared to concern her particularly and, although I was starting to wonder what on earth was wrong with Emma's knee, I did not see any point in voicing my fears, especially as she did not seem to have any herself. So we spent the weekend and the early part of the following week until my departure just going about our normal family life. This was mid-July, the children would soon be breaking up for their summer holidays, and we were looking forward to a whole six weeks ahead of us without the routine and strictures of school, bedtimes and early mornings. Although, thanks to the racing schedule, I would be away a lot, including virtually every weekend, the summer holidays were the most enjoyable time of year for us as a family because the children were around during the few days when I was at home during the week, so we could really make the most of the outdoor life with plenty of trips to the beach, wind-surfing, picnics, and barbeques with friends.

I left for Germany on the Wednesday, the day that Emma had to go for her scan. She had decided to take a friend with her, partly to keep her company and partly to take her mind off what she was going up there to do. After all, who ever likes going to a hospital?

3

Summer Holidays

EMMA'S BIRTHDAY FELL on 19 July, and I was planning to call her once I got back to the hotel a bit later that day, once I knew she would have seen Dr Flannery. It was only mid-morning in Germany, and therefore an hour earlier in England, so I thought that if I called her now, she might still be out doing the school run. Instead, I wandered around the paddock, thinking about where I might take up my position for the start of the qualifying sessions the next day. The German Formula 1 Grand Prix was in Hockenheim and, as was often the case with that particular race, which is known to be one of the hottest of the year, it looked as though it was going to be a scorching weekend. I was standing outside the Ferrari media centre's motorhome, already feeling the heat, when my mobile rang.

I was surprised to see our home number appear. I answered, but before I had had a chance to wish her happy birthday, Emma blurted out, 'Jon, it's a tumour. You've got to come home. I've just seen the doctor and he says it's a tumour. They don't know if it's malignant or not, so I need to have another scan and a biopsy. He says if you want to talk to him, you can.'

'Fine,' I replied, trying with difficulty not to sound completely shocked by what I was hearing. 'Fine. Look, don't worry, let me ring you back, I'm going to call the doctor.'

I hung up and felt for the first time that immediate throbbing, pounding of the heart, the sort that is so strong you can feel it in your throat; then a huge rush of adrenaline kicked in, and that feeling that I just wanted to spew my guts out there and then. Wasn't life great? One moment, everything is fine: here I am in the glamorous world of Formula 1, Michael Schumacher has just wandered past, and my beautiful wife is 35 today, happy birthday darling; the next, she's just told me she has a tumour, but they don't exactly know what sort it is; sorry, could you come in for some more tests and wait just a bit longer to hear your fate? At the best of times, the Formula 1 paddock is a pretty surreal experience, but now I had been hurled into a parallel universe of absurdity. And I must have looked like a total alien, because Sara, who had been in the car when I was driving to Bologna and had taken Emma's call after the initial X-ray, immediately spotted me and came over. 'Are you all right? You don't look too good.'

'Er, no,' I replied emptily. 'It's a tumour. Emma's got a tumour. I'm going to have to go home. Can I talk to you in a minute? I need to ring the doctor.'

I managed to get through to Mr Flannery, the consultant surgeon Emma had seen in Haslemere. He was obviously expecting my call, because everyone knows it's not usually that easy to get through to doctors of any kind. He was a young consultant and, in all our dealings with him, he always treated us with all the kindness that you could wish for in such difficult circumstances. 'Look, don't worry,' he tried to reassure me. 'This is the situation. We know it's a tumour, but it could be benign. It may not be malignant at all. If it's benign, we'll do . . .' Frankly, I was tuning out, I was no longer listening. He was trying to explain to me that they would do this if it was a benign tumour, but that if it was more 'sinister', as he put it, in other words, cancerous, they would do something else. '. . . so we need to assess it to know exactly how to treat it.'

After I had finished speaking to the doctor, I went straight over to speak to Becky, the girl at the company that organised all the travel for the Grand Prix circuit. 'I need to get a plane home tonight. Can you get me on the next BA flight?'

She looked up from her lunch. 'Do you have to go *now?*'

'Yes, Emma's not very well, seriously not very well, so I'm going to have to go home tonight.'

From my tone of voice, she immediately put down her sandwich, disappeared off for what seemed like an eternity, and returned looking rather gloomy. 'Sorry, Jon, I'm afraid the only BA flight out of Frankfurt today is at 4 o'clock, and you're not going to get there in time.'

That was it. Nothing doing. I was stuck in Hockenheim for the night.

I rang Emma back and told her I'd be back the next day. I tried to sound as calm as possible, because I didn't want her to feel that I was worried. Because if I was worried, she really would be, and would start to fall apart. Throughout our marriage, she relied on me to keep calm in situations that gave her cause for anxiety. She worried whether I would keep finding work, she worried when she miscarried the two successive pregnancies, she worried if the children had a fever. And each time, if I kept calm and reassured her, she would be fine. Now, more than ever, she needed to hear the right words from me.

I wandered around the paddock aimlessly for the rest of the afternoon, looking like a total zombie, surrounded by people I had known for 12, 14 years – photographers, journalists, all of them mates of mine – but unable even to acknowledge them. The circuit was free of cars and I remember at one stage walking out to the Armco, the barrier that goes round the side of the track, and just leaning on it, lost in thought. Or rather, I was so lost I didn't even have any thoughts. I was quite simply shell-shocked.

I resisted the urge to ring Emma a hundred more times that day, just to check whether she was okay, because I knew this would only make her panic all the more. I imagined her back home, looking after our three children, cooking them tea, reading them a story, putting them to bed that night; being a mother to them as she always was, rather than trying to bundle them off to bed early so that she could give free rein to her tears and anguish. She had probably rung a few friends to tell them, but, for the children's sakes, I am sure that she had carried on as usual. In that sense, Emma had a strength of character that was incredible. But deep down, I am equally sure that, that first night, she would have been worrying, panicking even. She might even have mentally rewound back to all those months, the year before, when her knee had been sore but she hadn't done anything about it. She might briefly have thought about the 'what if's. But she would have managed to push all those thoughts to the back of her mind, and carry on doing what she had to do. Indeed, that weekend, she and the kids were due to attend her brother's wedding. Some people might have made up some excuse and not gone. But not Emma. It was not in her make up. Nor would she ever have considered saying, 'Sorry to ruin your day, but I've just been told I've got a tumour, so I'm afraid I can't come to your wedding.' Until the day she died, nothing was going to stop her living her life as fully as she normally did.

Eventually, I went back to this ridiculous prefab hotel where I was staying, on the edge of the circuit. My room was a horrible, grim little box, with a sloping roof, the only source of daylight coming through a Velux window. The room was like an oven, because it had no aircon; outside it was stiflingly hot and there was not a breath of wind. I opened the window as wide as possible in an effort to cool down, but it made no difference: I could feel the sweat starting to pour off me. As I stared out of the window, I noticed that I looked straight out on to an aeroplane museum of some description. In front of me, as far as the eye could see, were planes of various sorts: Messerschmidts, twin propeller planes, even a grounded jumbo jet. In fact, there were planes everywhere. The irony was not lost on me as I tried to find ways of whiling away the hours until I could fly home. 'I know,' I thought to myself, 'since I didn't have time this morning, I'm going to have a shave. Just to take my mind off things.' So I had a shave. It didn't help. Then I had a shower, to try to cool me down, physically and mentally. The effect wore off almost at once. I tried to watch TV and flicked through until I got to CNN, then Eurosport, the only available English-language channels. But I couldn't concentrate on a thing.

Somehow, God knows how, the minutes ticked by and it was time to go for dinner. It was the last thing I felt like doing but I had agreed to go out for a beer and a pizza with some photographer friends of mine. I thought it might make me forget, even for a few minutes. They all sat there laughing and joking, ordering up more beers, munching hungrily through their pizzas. And I just sat there in silence. Eventually, Patrick, a mate of mine who was sitting at the other end of the table from me, sent me a text message. 'Are you okay?' it read. He didn't know what had happened – nor did any of those assembled.

I replied, 'Emma's not very well.'

'Oh, she'll be okay,' he texted back.

'She's NOT very well,' I sent back. 'I have to leave in the morning.' He looked at me, and I looked back. I couldn't stay a moment longer, got up to leave and took a cab back to the hotel.

Once there, I realised that, as this was mid-summer and Germany was an hour ahead of Britain, night would not fall until nearly 11pm. Thanks to the Velux blind, I didn't stand a chance of the room becoming dark until then. 'Oh my God,' I thought as I lay there staring up at this stupid, sloping roof in this ugly, hothouse room, 'I've just got to get some sleep. Somehow. I just want to be able to shut my eyes, wake up, and know that it's time to get out of this hell hole.' Eventually, I must have nodded off, only to be woken up at the crack of dawn by the light. I got up, shaved again, showered again, just to pass the time and went down to the circuit. At that time of the morning, there weren't many people around, but I collected some of my stuff and managed to find Sara and tell her to let the people know at Ferrari, for whom I was doing some photo-graphs, that I had had to leave urgently. There wasn't any need to lay it on with a trowel and do the big 'My wife has got a tumour' drama. I told a couple of other people that I bumped into – senior organisers of Grand Prix racing – that Emma was seriously ill, and that I had to go. But that was all they needed to know. They looked a bit stunned, but just wished me luck and a safe journey home. And with that I was off to the airport.

Frankfurt airport, like most airports, is a soulless, grey building. It feels dark inside, even though much of it is modern and built of glass. The drive to the airport felt interminable, as did the wait in the departure lounge. I paced up and down; I walked around the shops in a desultory way; I tried to read a newspaper. Once on board the plane, I sat in my seat, fidgeting and frustrated because I could not even call anyone on my mobile. The stewardess handed out a stale cheese roll and some bitter brown liquid she called coffee. Finally, we landed at Gatwick. I called the valet parking company so that they could bring my car round but when I dashed out of Arrivals, it still wasn't there. More pacing around as I waited for the car to appear. After what seemed like one of the longest journeys I had ever undertaken, I pulled up outside our house. Emma was sitting there waiting for me and she was clearly upset and worried.

I held her in my arms, and I asked her calmly, 'What's the situation?'

'Well, I've got to go to this hospital in Stanmore on Monday morning to have more scans and a biopsy.'

We didn't discuss the situation more than that. She asked me if I was coming to her brother's wedding, since I was home. 'No. Because I wasn't meant to be here anyway.' So Emma went on her own with the children. She looked fantastic, and no one had the faintest idea that anything might be wrong.

We got through the weekend. Business as usual. No what ifs. No discussing what we might do if this happened, or that.

What was the point? I have never seen the point in that sort of reasoning. What if the lights turn red just as I'm going through the crossing? What if I hit someone? What's the point? If I hit someone, *then* I'll deal with it. So I didn't want to start fast-forwarding to disaster scenarios. Why worry about something hypothetical? In the meantime, until I knew exactly what we were dealing with, I decided just to deal with what was in front of me: not letting Emma know that I was worried, carrying on as usual, and being with the children as I would normally be. We had never hidden anything from them, so they knew that their mummy's knee was not well. This time, we told them that we had to go back to the hospital to get it looked at, and they were too young to know what that might mean.

On the Monday, we got up early and took the kids over to some friends for the day before making our way to Stanmore, which is not far from Watford, north of London. The Royal National Orthopaedic Hospital is a major centre for all neuro-musculoskeletal problems, including care of those with acute spinal injury. It is also one of only two hospitals in the country that specialises in the care and treatment of patients suffering from advanced cancers of the bone. As I was to discover, they are leaders in limb salvage, a rather alarming term, which in Emma's case was to be of drastically important significance. The modern wing of the hospital houses paraplegics and tetra-plegics, all very injured people fighting to adapt to their new and terrible circumstances. Emma, meanwhile, had to go to an ugly wing round the back of the hospital which dated back to the start of the last century when the hospital was first built in its extensive grounds. Nissen huts were then installed during World War Two to house civilian casualties, and these, together with all the more recent additions to the original structure, have turned the hospital into its present-day jumble of buildings. None of that mattered, though, as we pulled into the car park. I didn't notice the surroundings at all. I simply had a tangible, physical realisation that, whatever it was that was wrong with Emma, we were going to be coming back here again.

The doctors and nurses did the full battery of tests on Emma, although I think they already knew what they would find. She had another MRI scan because it gives a 3-D perspective of bones and thus enabled the specialists to locate the exact epicentre of the tumour, find out the extent of the disease and whether it had spread since the previous scan. She also had a CT scan which took cross-section shots of various parts of her in order to show soft tissue such as muscles and lungs, because the latter in particular was where the secondary tumours would settle. Finally, the doctors did a core needle biopsy of her knee. Although it was done under local anaesthetic, it was still a very painful procedure for Emma to have a surgical instrument drilled several times straight into the middle of her joint and into the heart of the tumour so that bits of tissue could be retrieved for analysis.

The medical staff was very matter-of-fact. You don't see the consultants anyway, not at this stage. You see the radiographers, the nurses, the people who greet you with a kind smile and say, 'Hello, Emma, could you come this way?' before giving you a back-to-front robe that instantly dehumanises you and reduces you in one quick change of clothes to a faceless person, part of a conveyor belt of patients that they are testing that day. These medical people aren't going to tell you anything: they are not even going to let the slightest expression of worry cross their face as they say goodbye to you. It's not up to them to tell you what the tests reveal, even if they can see that there's some whopping great tumour staring them in the face as you pass down that tube. So again, there was no point in trying to ask myself any questions, or in trying to interpret whether they were saying goodbye to Emma in a 'Poor you, God, if only you knew' kind of way, or in a 'Well, that looks surprisingly encouraging' one. I was more concerned about how long we were going to have to wait in total for all these tests to be done, and how many copies of *Good Housekeeping* from five years ago I would have to wade through before tackling the two-hour drive home.

After a couple of hours, Emma hobbled back into the waiting room and we left. She just said that her knee was really sore, and that she was in a lot of discomfort. I didn't want to bombard her with questions that would simply remind her of what she had just gone through, and the emotional stress of the day meant that we were both tired, so we didn't talk much on the drive home. Then it was back to Haslemere, collect the kids, and carry on as normal. We were about to embark on the really dark, dark period of not knowing, of desperately trying to push away the darkest thoughts, of resisting the urge to press the fast forward button. Why torture ourselves?

We had been told that the results would be available later that week, but we decided to postpone returning to Stanmore until the following Monday: it was the school holidays and we had a summer holiday planned. As it was, we had already had to cancel our camping trip to France because the hospital had advised us to stay at home: the bone in Emma's leg out of which the tumour was growing was now so fragile that it could shatter at any moment, and the last thing we wanted was for this to happen in a foreign country where we did not speak the language. The thought of having to explain to French doctors what was wrong and having to repatriate Emma in such a situation just didn't bear thinking about. We had had to tell the children that there had been a last-minute change of venue for the holiday and initially they were really angry with us, as children usually are when they are too young to know that, sometimes, life doesn't go quite according to plan. But we were determined to give them at least one untroubled week away from home. That meant more to us than whether we got the test results back a few days earlier. So instead of disappointing the children even more by cancelling the holiday completely, we packed as soon as we got back from the hospital, set off late that afternoon and pitched our giant eight-man tent in a field that belonged to a friend of ours who lived in West Wittering in Sussex, not far from Chichester. By the time we started getting the sleeping bags out of the car, ready to settle down for the night, Emma and I were exhausted. One more test awaited us, however. Somehow, in our rush to leave, we had forgotten the children's pillows. And they were at an age where telling them to make a pillow out of the patch of grass they were lying on just wasn't going to work. So I got back in the car, drove all the way home, grabbed the three pillows and drove all the way back to where my family was waiting for me. It was late when we finally all curled up and went to sleep.

West Wittering has the most glorious beach, ideal for windsurfing, which I adore, and perfect for the kids to spend hours on, running around, building sandcastles, splashing around in the waves and generally burning off energy. Our week away coincided with the start of a heatwave across northern Europe, during which temperatures reached record highs – 40 degrees Celsius was recorded several days running in Paris – and, whilst it might have made life very unpleasant for city dwellers, for us it was idyllic. We spent the entire time outdoors, from the moment we woke up until the time we finally went to bed at night. Breakfast outside, picnics on the beach for lunch, and daily barbecues on the beach with friends who would come over for the evening. That week we lived as if we didn't have a care in the world. For the children, that was truly the case. For Emma and I, we didn't want to let on to each other or to the children that all was not well. I think Emma must have been absolutely terrified, despite her inner strength, but she was not showing it, and she was still functioning as if nothing was wrong. As for me, I would lie there, my mind often racing, but I would make a conscious effort not to let it run away with itself and freak me out. I would turn over, knowing that Emma wasn't sleeping either, and all I could do was whisper to her, 'Just wait, just wait.'

I was aware, though, that an almighty hurricane had now started to wind itself up. Ever since I had accompanied Emma to the hospital that Monday morning, I had got a real sense of its inescapable advance. I could see it coming closer; I knew it was going to hit us. The question was: with what force? My friend, whose field we were camping in, was a doctor – an eminent surgeon in fact – and he talked to me that week about what Emma had. Once I'd finished explaining to him what I knew, he said rather solemnly, 'You're going to need a lot of luck with this.'

'I know,' I replied, 'but we'll be okay.'

It was clear to me that Emma was now in a lot of pain. She would sit on the beach, try to walk down to the water, try to join in as much as she could, but she would often have to stop and tell the kids, 'I've got a sore knee. Carry on playing without me.' One evening, we had some friends over for a barbecue and, as I watched her walking across the field carrying Sam on her shoulders, I remember thinking to myself, 'God, she's really struggling.' But although she knew something was very wrong with her, at no time did Emma ever complain or start behaving like an invalid, expecting sympathy and assistance from those around her. She was utterly selfless in life, and she continued to be so throughout her illness.

4

The Diagnosis

Despite the hovering, growing anxiety, we had a wonderful holiday. Our last, it turned out, as a family of five. We came home on the Sunday, and, the next morning, had to go back to the hospital to hear once and for all what the doctors had to say about Emma's condition. In a now-familiar pattern, we got up early, dropped the children off at friends so that they could look after them for the day, and set off on the bleak journey that took us exactly halfway round the entire M25 and into Stanmore.

This time, Emma was very nervous in the car. She hardly said a word and sat there almost motionless while I tried to focus on the traffic. What was a two-hour trip felt as if we were crossing the Gobi desert: it was endless, hot and unpleasant. My heart was pounding. Every now and again, I would think of the reason why we were in the car, and instantly feel a burst of adrenaline pulsating through my entire body with such force that it made me want to gag. 'This is it,' I thought, 'this is the day when . . .' and immediately I knew I had to force my thoughts back down, bury them, not let them escape from the box where I tried to keep them. Speculation was pointless. And anyway, by the time the day was out, I'd know exactly what Emma was facing, and what lay ahead of us.

Eventually, we got to the hospital and were shown into the waiting room. It was crowded but we managed to find two plastic chairs next to each other and sat down in silence. Several people had various limbs in plaster. Many, in order to avoid catching anyone else's eye, were glancing idly through well-thumbed magazines marked 'Hospital Copy', but they weren't doing it because they were waiting to hear if they would live or die: they were simply bored and slightly unnerved, as everyone is, by a hospital waiting room. Emma and I were beyond being able to leaf through any magazines, or even say anything to each other. I just sat there numbly, wanting and not wanting this day to be over. Occasionally, everyone would look up expectantly when a nurse came in and called out a patient's name. Someone would get up and follow her out, then everyone else would cast their eyes back down and get on with whatever it was they were reading.

'Emma Nicholson?' Finally, it was our turn to be shown into the consultant's room. This was the NHS, not Harley Street, so there were no plush armchairs; just a small grey room, with a desk, more plastic chairs, and an examination couch. As we went in, I noticed that two women – one a nurse, one dressed in civvies – followed us in. That's when I knew the news would be bad. Why else would extra staff be parachuted in? The consultant, a strapping man called Mr Stephen Cannon, whom Emma and I had briefly met last time when she had come in to have the biopsy and scans, wasn't wearing a white coat, maybe because it was touchy-feely time. Not that I was conscious of this as it was happening, although I did understand, as soon as the two women walked in behind us, that the shit was about to hit the fan. Because they must get some people who absolutely freak out when they are told.

We shook hands with the doctor who welcomed us with a friendly smile, then we all sat down. I was shaking inside, just like you do when you're standing outside saying goodbye to someone, and it's winter and you haven't bothered to put your coat on because you think it'll be okay just for one minute. But then the goodbye takes a bit longer, and you can feel the chill start to grip you and you start to shiver. Thankfully the doctor got straight to the point; no point in doing the niceties. 'Hello, Emma. Well, we've got the results back, and I'm afraid you've got osteosarcoma, which is bone cancer.' Bang. Just like that. Hammer on the head, punch in the stomach. Call it what you will, it completely winds you; it doesn't matter how the blow is delivered.

Emma instantly crumpled in on herself and started to sob uncontrollably, with her head in her hands. The nurse, who had been sitting on the other side of Emma to me, put her arm around her gently. I came round from the body blow and thought to myself, 'Oh, I'd better put my arm around her,' so I did so and gave her a hug. But I was also aware that the doctor hadn't really finished his sentence, and that there was more to come. So although I was thinking, 'Cancer, cancer, cancer, oh my God,' I also sat up and listened to what he was about to say, because Emma was beyond that, and was just crying and crying, cradled in this woman's arms. 'We have scanned your chest,' he continued, 'and there are secondary tumours in both lungs.' He didn't say how many but I knew that secondary tumours were not good, in any shape or form, when it came to this disease. It meant that Emma would be chasing the cancer around her body until it finally caught up with her. Then, in a calm, clinical way, and without pausing to allow us to take in the enormity of what he had just said, the doctor delivered his verdict: 'And I'm not sure that I can treat you.'

At that moment, I knew Emma was dead. I remember just sitting there looking at him, speechlessly. I mean, what was there to say? 'Go on, say it,' I was thinking, 'get it over with and just tell her she's got three months to live!' But the other lady who had entered the room with us and who turned out to be our wonderful chemotherapy liaison person, Chris Henry, spoke up. 'I think you should try,' she suggested quietly, 'because they have three small children.'

Emma, meanwhile, at the mention of the word 'treat', started to rally a little and to sit up, wiping the tears away with the back of her hands, because for her, treatment meant getting better. I remember thinking that this was a slightly odd reaction, given the news she had just been given and how badly she had taken it just a few seconds earlier, but I wondered whether maybe she hadn't heard properly what Stephen Cannon had actually said. Had she heard him say, 'And I'm not sure I can treat you,' or had she just caught the end of that phrase and only heard the word 'treat'? In any event, the consultant contemplated the woman's words for a moment, weighing up what he thought he should do. Then he leaned forward a little and looked at Emma. 'Okay, here's what we're going to do: we're going to start you on chemotherapy as soon as possible, and we're going to give you the strongest combination of drugs that we can. *And*,' he emphasised very definitely, 'I want a response from the first bag. I want the pain to go.'

At that, Emma bounced back. She was back on, she was ready to fight. 'Oh, well, I don't have any pain,' she announced.

'What do you mean?' I said, turning in disbelief to the woman whom I had seen hobbling around in pain for the last few months. Trying to put on my bubbly, teasing, relaxed voice, I said, 'Hang on, you lie in bed with this pillow, whining about this, that and the other. What do mean you don't have any pain?' I was trying to defuse the horrendousness of the situation with the sort of jokey mock-insults that most couples go in for.

And the doctor added, as if anyone needed any more convincing, 'Look, you've got this huge tumour growing out of your thigh bone, the femur, and into the knee joint. The tendons and ligaments are under extreme pressure as a result, so you must have some pain. I know you're supermum, but you have got pain in your knee. And I need that pain to go in order to continue treatment.' And that was it. The ball was in Emma's court.

Mr Cannon then pressed on, hitting us with more facts and more information. Like many consultants, he was very matter of fact, and didn't have time to waste skirting around the truth. He wasn't going to stop and say, 'Sorry, I know this is difficult, do you want to have a tissue to wipe your nose while you get your head round what I have just told you?' He felt it was better to be honest and to give us the facts as far as we needed to know them at this stage. He knew the situation was dire, so although he wasn't brutal in the way he delivered the news, he moved swiftly on from one item to the next. 'You will now go and see Jeremy Whelan at the Middlesex Hospital in London. I work with him a lot and he will be in charge of your chemotherapy treatment. I know you're going to go away, do your research and think of getting a second opinion, but take it from me, you will discover that Jeremy Whelan is a total authority on your particular cancer, Emma, and you could not be in better hands. Later on, depending on how you react to the chemotherapy, we can look at the possibility of operating on your leg. But I have to tell you now that, in my opinion, there is a high probability that we will have to amputate.'

I was in shock. I had been hit so hard and with so much catastrophic news that I felt as if I was being shot at point blank range by a machine-gun and there was absolutely no chance that the guy with the gun was going to miss. Every single shot was going to hit the target: she's got cancer; she's got secondaries; they're not sure they can treat; they may well have to amputate her leg. And I had no choice but to sit there and take the bullets.

The doctor did some more talking, but really, what more was there to find out? Apart from discovering the minor detail that osteosarcoma is a childhood cancer that occurs in teenagers when their bones start to grow out of control. But in adults over the age of 25, it is so rare that it occurs in just two in every million people. So bad luck, really.

We were eventually shown out of the consulting room by the doctor. 'Everyone is going to know that we've just been given some really bad news,' I remember thinking, rather absurdly, as if that mattered, 'because Emma is still in a state and it's obvious she's been crying a lot.'

We crossed the waiting room and were shown into another small room, where Chris Henry, who had been so instrumental in obtaining treatment for Emma, sat down and talked us through the details of what would happen next. 'We're going to book you into the Whitbread ward at the Middlesex Hospital, which is in central London, Mortimer Street. You need to be ready for next Monday, and you're going to be an in-patient for four days, then you can go home for two days. You will then come back in for four days, and so on. You're going to come away from here and have a lot of questions, and I'm here to answer them . . .'

And so she continued, calmly and gently explaining every procedure, answering any questions, and trying to allay some of Emma's most urgent fears. Already, at that first meeting, I noticed that the balance had shifted and that she had talked almost exclusively to Emma. I was an irrelevance – or almost – and that was as it should be. Emma was the patient, the medical team's point of focus, the one with whom they would develop a close relationship as the weeks and months of treatment dragged on. This woman was wonderful, we were lucky to have her, and Emma came to rely heavily on her wisdom, her kindness and her ability to reassure her through her most difficult moments.

Finally, we were free to leave the hospital. As we got into the car, which had been sitting all afternoon in the blazing sun, it was as if we were getting into an inferno. On top of that, I was punch drunk, I had a searing headache, and I was completely dehydrated. Emma looked in an even worse state and was once again in tears. But for some strange reason, as I put the key in the ignition, I realised that I was smiling. Emma turned round and saw me. 'What are you looking so happy about?' she asked. For a moment, I thought she was going to hit me, and I wouldn't have blamed her if she had. 'Because we now know its name, we know what it is,' I tried to explain, even though I was taken aback that the weeks of uncertainty and the strange relief of finally knowing what we were dealing with were making me react like this. 'And I know what it is we've got to fight against. And *you* need to tell *it* that you know what it is, and that you're going to come after it. You've got to let it know that you're going to fight. Tell it, tell it. Because it's a foreign body.' Emma just looked at me, slightly bemused, and just mumbled, 'Right, yes. You're right.' Then she sat back in her seat, and didn't say another word until we were almost home.

For me, though, as I crawled back round the M25, those words, 'And I'm not sure I can treat you,' 'And I'm not sure I can treat you,' kept going round and round in my head, like some sort of endless echo, quickly followed by, 'Fuck, this woman is going to die, this woman is going to die.' I tried desperately to concentrate on the busy road and to calm down, to think more coolly about what lay ahead, rather than give in to panic and despair. Although in a way I was relieved that the long, excruciating wait for the results was over, I now knew that this was going to get brutally ugly, and that we were not going to have a happy ending. I had to accept that Emma was going to die.

I realise not everyone in my situation would have reacted with my certainty but I had heard enough to know what the outcome of Emma's illness was going to be. After all, how much clearer can a doctor be when he says, 'And I'm not sure I can treat you,' given that it is a doctor's absolute duty to do whatever he can to treat people? Also, coming from a family of medics – my father had been a doctor, and my sister now was – I had enough medical knowledge to understand that once you have secondary tumours, especially in tissue such as the lungs, nothing, bar a miracle, is going to save you. It was therefore not a defence mechanism which made me accept defeat from the outset, nor hard-heartedness, nor pessimism, but rather the pragmatic acknowledgement of the medical reality of the situation. If another doctor had been given that diagnosis, he or she would also have known, and although I am no doctor, I knew enough about Emma's condition to be sure of what awaited her. I didn't know how long it would take, nor what would happen along the way, but I knew that whatever treatment she tried would simply be prolonging her life, rather than saving it.

My task now was to give Emma all the support I could, not let on that I knew she was going to die, but be there to give her what she needed from me in order to make what remaining time she had left as bearable and normal as possible, both physically and psychologically. I had to help her get through whatever lay ahead of her. As for the children . . . I tried not to focus too much on what awaited us, but I knew that I had to be absolutely rock solid for them. That was going to be the most important thing. And I would do whatever it took in order for them to survive their mother's illness with as little damage as possible.

No one or nothing ever prepares you for this sort of situation, and I had a slightly sick feeling in my stomach at the thought that I might not be up to what would be required of me, and that I might fail to support and help my wife and children just when they needed me the most. I realised immediately that all notions of me going away to work, of relying on Emma to run the house and look after the kids, of knowing that my children ran to their mother first whenever they needed a plaster or a cuddle, all these and a million other things would have to change. And change almost from the moment we got back.

It also dawned on me, as I wove my way through the traffic, that once Emma actually died, I was going to have to change lanes. My life as I had known it would be a thing of the past. And I knew that, in the time Emma had left, I had to prepare myself really well for moving into what was clearly going to be the fast lane, so that once I was there, I could make damn sure I didn't crash. My children's welfare depended on it.

Emma ended up drifting off to sleep in the car, while I spent the rest of the journey listening to music in an attempt to get myself in the right frame of mind to go and collect the kids. As a result, by the time we got home later that afternoon, Emma and I had not had a chance to discuss how or what to tell them. But we both knew instinctively that we had to tell them the truth – or at least the truth as Emma understood it. Clearly, I wasn't going to tell them that their mother was going to die, but they should at least know that their mother was ill, that she had cancer, and that the doctors were going to do all they could to make her better. If you explain things to children in a language that they understand, in an almost matter-of-fact way, they are more than able to accept the information and to cope. They treat the news in a different way from adults who bring a whole lot of baggage with them: previous experience of the illness through other people who have had it, media coverage of it, layman's knowledge of it (a little knowledge can do a lot of harm) and an instinctive terror of the word cancer. 'The Big C' it's often called euphemistically, and in an attempt to inject some humour into the term. Fortunately, children have usually not lived long enough for experience to have instilled in them a fear of that word. Also, they take their parents for granted: it doesn't occur to them that they are mortal. Parents are just there, end of story. Until that day when experience teaches them otherwise.

I collected Molly, Maisy and Sam from our friends up the road, dropped them back at the house and went straight out again to Tesco because I hadn't yet had time to restock the fridge after our week away. I parked the car and was about to get out when I realised I felt the need to call Damon Hill, someone who would understand just a little bit what it was like to receive difficult, painful news. Damon, for all his fame and success, has had some tough things happen in his life, not least the death of his father in a plane crash when Damon was still a boy. I managed to get hold of him on his mobile because I knew he was on holiday in Spain. I was in a state of disbelief about the entire day, so it felt very surreal to be sitting in a Tesco's car park, talking to Damon, who was no doubt sunning himself by a pool, saying, 'Look, I'm really sorry to ruin your holiday, but we've just had the results and Emma's got cancer.' I carried on and told him what we knew and, although he knew that Emma had been unwell and had undergone tests, he was still shattered to hear the diagnosis. He promised to come over when they got back the following week and I hung up soon after, because I didn't want to be away from home for too long.

I dashed round the aisles, and, in my hurry to get out as quickly as possible, grabbed anything off the shelves that seemed even vaguely useful. I was aware that Emma was back home with the children, and that we would have to tackle the issue of telling them the news. By the time I got back less than an hour later, I immediately sensed that something had changed. As I heaved half a dozen carrier bags out of the boot, I was greeted by Molly, who was only 10 but was already showing all the signs of being a chip off the old block, in other words, a bit of ranter, like me, who flew off the deep end at the slightest opportunity. She was gabbling away frenziedly and I couldn't make out what she was on about. 'Hang on, be quiet, be quiet, calm, down. What's going on? What's wrong?' I asked, as I heaved the bags on to the kitchen counter. 'What do you mean?' she asked, sounding a bit like a young Lady Bracknell. 'I've just lost my purse, my mother's got cancer? How do you think I feel?' That was Molly, in a nutshell. Instant drama, and at that precise moment, the lost purse was as much of a disaster as her mother getting cancer.

Emma had clearly told them. I don't know what she had said, but she'd obviously decided to tell them straight away, without waiting for me. Although we hadn't decided what we were going to say, we had both agreed we would tell the children the next day, together. Something had obviously happened to change all that. 'What's going on?' I asked, as I went in to the kitchen and saw Emma sitting at the kitchen table. 'I had to tell them. I had no choice.' She then told me that, while I was out, she had wanted to give Sam a cuddle but, as she cradled him in her arms, he had suddenly looked at her and said, 'You're not my mummy anymore.'

'What do you mean? Of course I'm your mummy!' she had said, trying to sound all casual and light hearted. Sam, who was only four and a half at the time, but who was already a very sharp, articulate little boy, had gone on, in that way that children have of making the most piercingly accurate comments about people and of saying the unspeakable, 'No you're not. Your face is all flat.'

'After that,' Emma explained, 'I knew I couldn't wait. I had to tell them the truth there and then.'

5

No Time for Adjustment

We had just been taught one of our first lessons when it came to this illness: it was almost impossible to plan anything. You have to be ready to jump when the gun goes off, and you never know when that might be. There is no time for adjustment, no time to rehearse a situation. Things happen, you don't know what or when, and you just have to deal with them. One thing we did know, however, and even without explicitly discussing it between us, was that we were going to be honest with our children from the start. After my own experience with my father's death, I knew I did not want the children to be kept in the dark about their mother's illness. We had always tried to communicate as much as possible with them, to talk to them and explain things to them, so we didn't see why we should suddenly start to be secretive about what was happening. Not only would it have been almost impossible to hide from them that their mother was soon going to be very ill from the treatment she was going to receive, but also if they discovered we had lied or hidden from them the nature of the illness, why would they ever want to trust us again? And I, as the surviving parent, would inevitably be the one suffering the consequences of my children's loss of trust.

Nothing more was said that day about Emma's illness. Everyone carried on as normal: Emma was determined to continue being their mother, as if nothing had changed, and the children didn't discuss the matter any further. There was shell shock all round but no one sat around in a big heap crying their eyes out. We didn't want to frighten the children any more than they might already have been, so we tried to make the rest of the day as enjoyable as possible. Nonetheless, Sam – who had been dry at night for a few months – did wet the bed that night. And he continued to wet the bed every single night thereafter for the next 14 months. In fact, he didn't stop until the night after Emma died.

Over the next few days, the children would occasionally ask Emma what was going to happen and she would try to explain as clearly as possible. 'I'm going to have this treatment, and my hair is going to fall out,' and, whenever she could, she would make the answers positive and upbeat. But gradually, the children started to ask me questions as well. 'Why is Mummy going to get sicker when she's already sick?' 'What is cancer?' Often, I found that it helped to explain the situation visually, with the use of drawings to accompany my words. This was especially important because I had to tailor what I said to each child, because what Molly was able to understand in terms of sheer complexity of vocabulary was clearly going to be different from what Maisy could, and what Maisy could understand would differ again from what Sam could grasp. Drawings were a good way to ensure that all three of them could follow what was going on. So I drew where the tumour was, I drew the good cells and the bad cells. I drew the medicines that Mummy was going to take and how they were going to kill the bad cells. But

I also explained that the treatment was going to have to kill some good cells as well as the bad cells and that the doctors would make her really sick before they could hopefully make her better. And usually, explaining the situation with the use of drawings and clear words was enough to reassure the children and ensure that they understood not only what was happening but also why.

These chats soon became known as the 'Daddy chats' and they became the main method of making sure that my children never became confused or worried about what was happening. It was a way for them to feel they could open up and ask me anything, and they could also tell me about anything that was making them sad or anxious. The Daddy chats were never a formal thing. I didn't suddenly decide one day that we were going to institute a system of official 'chat times'. They grew naturally out of the fact that I was incredibly aware that each child absolutely had to know what was happening, and had to have an outlet for their fears or unhappiness. Sometimes all the children would be sitting together with me, but more often than not, I'd be in the kitchen, for example, and one or other of them would ask me something, or be sad or upset, and I would say, 'Right, let's go upstairs and have a Daddy chat.' Off we'd go for a bit of privacy, and I would not finish the Daddy chat until I felt the issue that had been bothering that child had been resolved.

Whilst Emma was still waiting to start her treatment, the children tended to ask her the questions, but I noticed that as soon as she started it, they shifted and confided in me instead, and that is when the Daddy chats really started in earnest, because on the days when she did come home, they were just happy to have their mum back. They didn't want to start asking her difficult questions, or confide in her about their darkest fears, particularly when they saw how ill the treatment soon made her.

A couple of days after the diagnosis, we had the first visit from the district nurse. Initially, she came to run through the paperwork and the logistics of how she was going to work with the oncology team at the Middlesex, but she also took some blood samples to establish, amongst other things, exactly what Emma's white blood count was, and to determine whether it was high enough to enable her to go into hospital for her next session of chemo. The blood tests enabled liver function to be tested as well. The district nurse paid us a daily visit at 9.30 sharp whenever Emma was at home. She became part of our lives, part of our daily routine, and, on the odd occasion when she was late, her absence made us, and Emma in particular, feel extremely vulnerable and anxious.

Emma had been diagnosed on the Monday. By the Thursday, I had packed my bags and flown off to the Hungarian Grand Prix that weekend. I was contractually obliged to go, I was being paid well for it, and I could not let Olympus down. Luckily, there hadn't been a race for the previous three weeks, and this had allowed us to have our short holiday together. It had also enabled me to be with Emma for her last two trips to Stanmore. From now, though, until the end of the season in mid-October, there would be races every two weeks. And I was going to have to cover them, whether I liked it or not. All we could do was to make sure that Emma's parents and our friends who lived locally were able to help out whenever I was away, knowing that from November onwards I would not be going away for work until the following spring.

Emma was booked in to start her chemotherapy treatment only 10 days after she had been given her diagnosis, so she decided, during that time, to anticipate the inevitable and buy herself a selection of scarves. She ended up with a wide array of possible headgear: everything from silky, multicoloured Hermès scarves to cheap but no less colourful high street numbers. She was able to joke about it but she knew exactly what all these scarves represented.

In the meantime, I took delivery of a car that I had ordered some weeks before, in another life, when we did not yet know that cancer would be our sole focus for the foreseeable future. I had traded in an unwieldy Japanese people carrier for a Mini, a car I had always loved and which I thought would be a useful run-around when I went off on all my many trips. We still had a Renault Scenic that we used when we had to drive the children around, so the Mini was never meant to be the family car. But when I pulled up outside the house in my new car, Emma took one look and simply walked away. 'Well, how do you expect to get everyone around in that?' she threw at me over her shoulder.

It was my birthday during this time, and again, some weeks before, I had managed to get hold of a pair of tickets to go and see the Rolling Stones at Wembley. Even if Emma hadn't been ill she wouldn't have gone, because she wasn't a great fan. But I was, so I was determined to go, despite the situation, and asked Damon to accompany me now that he was back from holiday. I suppose I did manage to enjoy the concert, but I also felt totally alienated from what, for everyone else, was an electric atmosphere and buzz. Everything around me felt as if it was going on in a sort of utterly weird, parallel universe. I remember sitting there thinking throughout, 'Shit, this is unreal, here am

I listening to my all-time favourite band, and my wife's got cancer.' Damon kindly offered to get us backstage, but I didn't want that: partly because this was my treat, I'd got the tickets, and I wanted us to be here like normal fans, not as Damon Hill and his mate; and partly because, frankly, there was no way I felt up to that. I was still in a state of deep shock. Now was not exactly the time to meet my idols Mick and Keef.

The next day, there was almost no mention of how my evening had gone, just a cursory, rhetorical 'Good evening?' from Emma, which demanded a low-key, throw-away reply from me. I didn't feel I could say, 'Oh my God, the Stones were ab-so-lu-tely great! Keith was fantastic,' then proceed to enthuse for the next half hour about just how fabulous my night out had been. Here was a woman who had just been diagnosed with cancer and was about to start on a gruelling, desperate fight for her life. Understandably, she wasn't very interested in my evening in London watching a band she wasn't mad keen on, just as she wasn't exactly bowled over by the appearance of my new Mini. On the other hand, I was slightly frustrated that, however appalling Emma's situation was, I was now being made to feel bad for any brief moment of enjoyment. I wasn't expecting her to be very interested or to want to ask excitedly about every detail of the concert. But I would have liked some sort of acknowledgement that she was glad that I had had a good time. It is very difficult for those who care for people who are seriously ill or dying. They often feel – or are made to feel – guilty about having some time for themselves, about enjoying themselves, about laughing. Some people think that, because the patient is having a shit time, all those caring for them should have a shit time as well. Everyone should suffer together.

Yet I see no logic in that. I am not advising carers to go dancing around the patient, exclaiming gleefully how much fun they are having or have had. But nor do I see the point in carers dragging themselves down by denying themselves some respite from what is always an extremely demanding situation. I was a human being, not just a carer, and I firmly felt that if I didn't sometimes take time out for myself, to recharge my batteries, I would not be of any help either to Emma or to the children. In order to stay strong for them, I had to allow myself some time on my own, both through work and through pleasure. And I do believe everyone in my situation should be able to do that if they want – or need – to.

Emma's reaction to the Mini and to the Rolling Stones concert started to sow some seeds of frustration on my part regarding her illness and what it was going to do to us. It is quite possible that it may have sown some similar seeds in her mind as well. In any event, I sensed that this was but the start of what lay ahead: cancer does things to people and affects them in ways that you would never think possible. You are warned about the physical effects of the disease. What you are not warned about is the way in which it also eats away at all relationships. Whatever the eventual outcome of the illness, no relationship is left unaffected. And I was not prepared for that when Emma first became ill.

One of the biggest tasks facing us at this time was having to tell those closest to us what was wrong with Emma. Tellingly, I have no memory of telling my mother or sisters, though I clearly must have done so at some stage. But it fell to Emma to tell her parents that their youngest child, their only daughter, to whom they were very close, had osteosarcoma. I was not privy to the actual conversation, but it is not hard to guess that they would have been devastated. They would have maintained a stiff upper lip, because that is what they are like, but they would have been unspeakably upset and grief stricken, particularly as Emma had played down over the previous months the problems she had been having with her knee. Whenever they spoke on the phone, not wanting to worry them, she had not mentioned that she was having a multitude of tests done. When they saw her and noticed that she was limping, she had simply answered breezily, 'Oh it's nothing, I think it's some ligament damage from when I fell back in the winter. It'll eventually go away.' Now, inescapably, she had had to tell them.

Meanwhile, I sat down and slowly made my way through the list of other people who had to be told: mainly friends from the children's school, and close friends of mine and Emma's, many of whom knew that she had been having tests. I couldn't help noticing that the last time I had done a mass ring round to friends and family had been after the birth of each of our three children. Then, the news had been happy, and I'd been delighted to call as many people as I could. Now, I was at the opposite end of the news spectrum and I couldn't wait to get off the phone. Eventually, I started to say to people, 'Look, do you mind telling X or Y,' or 'I'm sorry, I've got a lot of people to talk to, so can I just tell you briefly . . .' But even then, X and Y would inevitably call later on, and I – rather than Emma – would have to speak to them to explain what the situation was, and even the brief conversations took longer than I wanted because people naturally asked questions.

I also realised that I needed to speak to Molly's new school – Midhurst Intermediate – where she was about to start a few days later. Because they didn't know Molly at all, they had no idea, unlike Maisy's primary school (which Molly had just left), that Emma was even unwell. So I turned up one morning just before the start of the new school year, and asked to see the head-mistress. 'Well, we don't normally see parents before the start of term . . .' the headmistress began by saying when I had finally tracked her down. 'I know, but I'm afraid I have to sit down and talk to you,' I insisted, politely but firmly. So she showed me into her office, slightly alarmed at what I might be about to tell her and I explained to her about Emma. 'It's not a great situation, and it's not going to end happily. Molly does not want to be treated any differently, but I wanted you to be aware that if she suddenly throws her pencil case across the classroom, she might be doing it because there's a fair amount of stress going on in her life right now.'

Although Molly had not wanted me to go in and talk to the school, the headmistress was glad I had told her. 'It's important that we know this sort of thing about a child,' she had assured me. Fortunately, throughout her two years there, the teachers never mentioned to Molly that they knew, never made an issue out of the situation, and treated her like any other pupil. And Molly, in turn, threw herself into work as soon as she started there, using the school as a place where she did not have to think about what was going on at home. It was a refuge of normality. She didn't want to stand out from her friends by being different – or not in that way, at least. In fact, as far as I know, Molly never spoke to her friends about her mother's illness during the entire time that she was at that school.

As Stephen Cannon had predicted, in the days following the diagnosis I had indeed started to do some research about osteosarcoma and about the oncologist, Jeremy Whelan, who would now be looking after Emma at the Middlesex. Through medical connections, I soon discovered that he was indeed Mr Osteosarcoma and that we could not have a better expert on the subject. Going privately was going to make no difference because he only worked on the NHS. It is a common misconception that going private is inevitably better and quicker, but for us, that would definitely not have been the case. We were seen as quickly as it was possible to do so, and Emma received the best treatment she could, given her diagnosis. We were fortunate to have Jeremy Whelan because knowing that we were in the best hands was essential for Emma's mental well-being. Indeed, being fully confident about their medical team is something that all cancer patients should be entitled to.

As for finding out more about her particular cancer – cancer being a layman's umbrella term for dozens of different forms of the condition – I started trawling the Internet on the very first evening after we got back from Stanmore. It's fair to say that on my first click of the mouse, I realised just how much rubbish there was to wade through in cyberspace when it came to cancer. It's really a question of how cranky do you want to go? That first evening, I got confirmation of a few basic facts, and left it at that, because I was in no mood for some of the insane material on offer that is targeted to exploit vulnerable, desperate people. Plus, I already knew that our oncologist was the best, so I postponed further research until I felt calmer and clearer about the whole situation, and until Emma had actually started her treatment. Only after that would we know whether they would even continue with the chemo, and therefore what her short-term future was.

~

Ten days after seeing Stephen Cannon in Stanmore and being told that he wasn't sure that he could treat her, Emma began her chemotherapy at the Middlesex Hospital. It had been explained to her that she would be on the most brutal regime that it was possible to give someone, and that it was not without risk, the risk being that the drugs might kill her before the tumour did. The plan was to continue this treatment – assuming that she responded well to the first session – for approximately six months. Some time during this period, and again, depending on how she responded, the doctors might look at operating on the tumour in her knee in order to remove the primary site. But that was a very long way off. The main aim now was for Emma to get through her chemo, which was by no means a certainty.

Emma and I set off on the first morning by car for central London. The Middlesex Hospital has since closed down, and at the time it was already in a shocking state. In fact, it seems incredible that it could get away with treating such seriously ill people, given the condition it was in. It wasn't so much the dirt I noticed as the sheer dilapidation: paint was peeling off the walls and the ceilings, and it had the air of being old and totally run down. Emma, in contrast, was totally up for it. In fact, she was positively champing at the bit. Standing by the small side entrance to the hospital in Nassau Street, we looked at each other before going in. No words were needed, but we both had that 'Right, let's get on with it' look in our eyes. Not in a grimly negative way, but rather in a way that entailed rolling up our sleeves and standing up to whatever lay ahead.

Up the stairs we went, turned left and, as we pushed open the wooden swing doors and entered the chemotherapy wards, Emma looked at me once more and said, 'And now the fight begins.' A corridor separated the men's ward on the right from the women's ward, the Whitbread ward, on the left. This would now be her home for most of the next six months. But as soon as we entered, Emma stopped. She became rooted to the spot as she became aware of all these figures sitting or lying there, as far as the eye could see. What she saw was like a scene from the Western Front: all were women, all were clearly ill, but some looked barely human. Suddenly, the realisation of where she was suddenly hit Emma. It was as if she had suddenly been winded. 'Oh my goodness,' she whispered, defiance still audible in her tone, 'I'm never going to look like these people!' 'Yes you are, my love,' I thought to myself, 'because you may not realise it yet, but I'm afraid that's what chemotherapy does to people.'

Emma had never come face to face with anyone who looked so shockingly ill; now she was staring at maybe 20 of them. She might briefly have been destabilised by what she had seen but, being Emma, her inner strength immediately took over once again. 'Right, where's my bed,' she started asking as soon as the sister and the nurse in charge came to greet us. Both were lovely and were great at immediately settling her in.

Before long, she was sitting on the bed, having unpacked the small bag she had brought with her containing the bare essentials: nightwear, washbag, a book and a notepad and pen. 'If you want to go now, that's fine,' she said, smiling at me. She seemed perfectly calm and I was struck at how she appeared to be taking everything in her stride. Like many people, I hated hospitals. The ward felt hot and oppressive, and the sight of all these dehumanised women had unsettled me, because I knew that I was leaving my wife behind to suffer treatment that would undoubtedly, in time, leave her looking like those around her. 'Right, okay, I'll give you a ring later on.' I kissed her goodbye, got the number of the ward from the nurse, and walked out of the ward.

As I was about to exit, I turned around one last time to wave to my gorgeous, precious wife whom I was leaving behind for four long days to endure treatment that would ravage every inch of her body. And I remember distinctly that, as I looked behind me, the only thing that stood out from the whole scene was Emma's glorious hair. It was a vivid detail amongst a sea of blur. It's like when you walk into a room but don't see anything specific at first. Then, after a second, your eyes fix on one salient element. Emma's mane of curly hair was that one element which immediately stood out: simply because she was the only one who still had hair.

Jolted by what I had seen, I got back in the car but quickly realised I didn't have time to sit around with my mind in turmoil. I had to get back to Haslemere to collect the children from the friends who were looking after them. So it was left down Tottenham Court Road and straight on with running the house on my own for the next few days. I knew I was perfectly capable of looking after my children on my own. I was lucky not to have an office job that took me into work for long hours every day, 45 weeks of the year, and in the past, whenever I had been at home, I had been very involved in my children's lives and in the running of the house. But this time it was different: the routine started and stopped with me, and I knew I had to get it right, because there was no one else to pick up any pieces if I messed up.

Thanks to good advance planning on the part of Emma and me, everything went smoothly during those four days. The children were still off school and were kept busy with friends, so they seemed generally unperturbed by their mother's absence. The Daddy chats had begun in earnest, which undoubtedly helped as well, and kept their fears at bay, and, before long, it was time for me to go and collect Emma from the hospital. As we discovered, though, once Emma came home after that first bout of treatment and promptly went neutrapenic within a few hours, any notion we had that we could settle into some sort of regular pattern of four days in hospital, two days at home, had quickly evaporated. We learned yet again that there was no such thing as routine with this illness, and we had to grasp the good moments when they came because we never knew when there might be another.

By the time Emma came home after her second session of chemo, I could tell that the drugs were starting to have an effect. And not just a minor one: it was as if a nuclear reactor was going off inside her. Not only had the pain in Emma's knee gone after the first session, as the doctors had wanted in order to continue treating her, but her skin was also starting to look grey and pale. Most obviously, though, her once abundant hair was now beginning to fall out. If she ran her hand through it, she wouldn't just be left with the odd hair in her fingers, as a normal, healthy person would. A handful of strands would effortlessly be left behind.

That evening, with the kids safely tucked up, I was downstairs clearing up after dinner while Emma was upstairs in bed. After a while, thinking she may have fallen asleep, I tip-toed upstairs, but saw that the light was still on in our room.

I went in, to be confronted by Emma sitting up in bed, barely recognisable: using my clippers, she had quietly cut off all her hair, shearing it right off, as short as she possibly could. My heart missed a beat; I was in complete shock. How the hell could she just go and do that? Before I could utter a word, she said to me in a matter-of-fact way, 'It was going to fall out anyway.' I knew she was right, and I was in awe of her courage, of her act of sheer bloody-minded defiance. By cutting off all her hair, she was basically saying to the disease, 'I know *you* are going to make me ugly, but I'm going to show you. I'll get there before you get to me.' But for me, seeing her like this was a moment of the most appalling, sickening sadness, and I was furious. Not at Emma. But I was furious that this mutilation – for that is how it felt to me – of her incredible hair, of a part of her that so defined her, had shattered the fragile, precarious normality that I was still desperately trying to cling to. I knew it was just a question of time until the cancer took its toll on her appearance, but until that moment, I could still look at Emma and think that she didn't yet look ill. Now, there she was, lying in our bed, looking like the archetypal cancer patient. That was a defining moment in her illness, because this was a physical manifestation of the fact that there was no reverse gear. This was just the beginning of how cancer was going to change Emma for ever.

The next morning, I worried about the children's reaction to seeing their mother look so different: would they be upset? Frightened, even? Although they had been told that she would lose her hair, I didn't know how they would be affected when confronted by the actual reality. Incredibly, they thought she looked anything but scary, and I think this was in part due to the lack of fear we had so far managed to instil in them regarding their mother's illness. Molly and Maisy just couldn't stop cooing over her number one haircut. 'Oooh, oooh, look!' they kept repeating, as if it was just a weird new look. Sam's reaction, though, was the most extraordinary: sitting next to his mother on the bed, he kept running his little hand over her head, saying, 'Oooh, that's so nice and soft, Mummy!' I suppose he was right: it *was* like velvet. Not for the first time, Sam's young age had enabled him to speak from the heart, with total honesty, and without fear of saying the wrong thing.

6

Dark Days

FROM THAT MOMENT on, the treatment started to maul Emma's body. I don't doubt that it temporarily halted the spread of the many tumours that were growing inside her – we still didn't know how many – but every time she came back from the hospital she was visibly sicker than when she had gone in. As well as her hair coming out in clumps, revealing increasing sections of bare scalp, all other body hair began to fall out as well. Her skin began to take on the pallor and fragility of porcelain, and to look parched and starved of any life. They say that cancer treatment makes a person more ill than the cancer itself, which is true, but never is that more shockingly apparent than when that person was previously young, fit and beautiful.

Sometimes, Emma was too unwell to be allowed home. Her drug regime was brutal, relentless, and involved her taking three different chemotherapy drugs over a five-week cycle. On days one and three of her four-day stay, two drugs called Doxorubicin and Cisplatin would be administered intravenously via what is called a Picc line. The drugs would then be flushed out, as well as on days two and four, with fluids containing a mix of salt and sugar. On days five and six, Emma would hopefully be allowed home. The same pattern would be repeated twice more. Then, on days 22 and 29, only one drug, methotrexate, would be given, followed by three days of flushing out, because that drug was so immensely toxic. That would complete the pattern of five bouts of chemotherapy, and after that, the whole cycle would begin again. The plan was to continue over a six-month period and hope that the treatment didn't kill her in the meantime. Each time she went into hospital, Emma would have the full battery of tests: she would have an MRI scan to see how the primary tumour in the knee was responding, and chest X-rays and CT scans of her lungs to monitor what was happening to the secondary tumours there. In addition, Emma's blood would be tested both before and after the drugs were pumped into her, to see if her immune system was strong enough to enable her to leave hospital. And sometimes, unsurprisingly, it wasn't. She would go neutrapenic as soon as she arrived, and would have to be blasted with antibiotics until she was able to resume the chemo. On other occasions, I would get a call from her on the morning when I was supposed to collect her, telling me that her white blood count wasn't high enough. 'Are you going to be able to come home?' I would ask, in hope. 'Well, they're going to test me again at four o'clock to see. I'll have to call you back.' And I would immediately be thinking, 'Okay, but the kids are back from school at that time. I'm going to have to call in favours and make alternative arrangements now, so that I can drive up to London and pick you up. And I'll have to explain to the kids why their mum isn't at home when they get back from school as they hoped she would be.'

Another regular problem was that the veins into which the drugs were pumped were liable to collapse. And if that happened, treatment would be stopped, which was very troubling for Emma. So the nurses would struggle to find a vein that wasn't already so weakened by the treatment that it could hold up for the next few days. Every available vein in her arms, hands, and feet were eventually used, and at one stage, the Picc line – the most vital component of her treatment – was inserted directly into a vein in her chest. On another occasion, she had her arm in a splint so that it wouldn't dislodge the fragile vein that was on the verge of collapse. As a result, she was unable to move her arm for a few days, and had to be extra careful when anyone approached her.

Sometimes, it wasn't a question of Emma not coming home, but rather the reverse: the hospital would call on the morning that she was due to come in, to inform her that 'Terribly sorry, but we don't have a bed. Can you phone us this afternoon to see if we can admit you?' That would upset her, and in many ways it was outrageous, but it wasn't the hospital's fault. They tried really hard, but the simple truth was that another patient's blood levels had prevented them from going home, there were only so many beds on the ward, and that was that. There was nothing we could do except wait.

Life was now a pattern of endless chaos, and of having to react to that chaos. My days, when Emma was in hospital, which was most of the time, involved getting the children up and ready for school. Sam, in particular, still needed help getting dressed, and they all needed packed lunches. Then, at 8.06am, very precisely, I would bundle them into the car. First, Molly would be dropped off in Midhurst, six miles away, because she had to be in school by 8.20. Then I would double back and drive to Maisy and Sam's infant and primary school in Fernhurst, which is just three miles from Haslemere. The doors didn't open until

8.45, so we would always have a precious 10 or 15 minutes to sit in the car, chatting or listening to music – theirs or mine, *Grease*, the Rolling Stones, Neil Young, it just depended on what we felt like that morning. Sometimes, the kids would simply lean over from the back seat to hug me in silence for several long minutes. As soon as they went off, I would shoot back home, tidy up the breakfast things, make the beds, then sit down and call Emma to make sure she was okay. Luckily, the phone situation was quite straightforward in the Whitbread ward: I would call a number, and they would wheel that phone to her bed. After speaking to Emma, I would get on with some housework, put a wash on, then go off to the shops to buy whatever was needed.

As I had always been involved with the running of the house, I suppose I had to count myself fortunate that I didn't feel hopelessly and utterly lost when it came to managing on my own. Okay, so I had forgotten the yogurts, once, but I never forgot them again, though, of course, I forgot other things. Sometimes, especially at the beginning, I would go off to buy something specific, would end up buying all sorts of other things, only to come home and realise I'd forgotten the one thing we really needed. Or I'd walk into the supermarket, start at one end, go up and down every single aisle, take everything I thought we needed, and end up nine times out of 10 with about 500 loo rolls under the stairs, because I didn't actually need to buy loo rolls every single time I went shopping. So I learned. And now, of course, I can just skim past the shelves, pick out whether we need something and throw it in the trolley.

By the time the house was in order, there wasn't much time to do anything else other than catch up on phone calls or emails, because I had to set off again at 2.45 sharp in order to meet Molly off her school bus which dropped her in Fernhurst at 3pm. She'd get in the car and that was when we could have our own time together until the younger two came out of school at 3.30. Back home, Molly would do her homework, Maisy would have a bit as well, and Sam might have a bit of reading. Once that was out of the way, the children would then call Emma and I would start to make their tea. Nothing too complicated, but I did try and cook them something reasonably nourishing. Sunday was when I really pushed the boat out: a roast for lunch, accompanied by plenty of epically crispy roast potatoes. We also had a wonderful friend, Lisa Middleton, who made us mind-blowingly good lasagne twice a week, which we gobbled up every time with enthusiasm. On a practical level, knowing that twice a week I wouldn't have to take time out from the frantic evening routine of tea, bath, bed, story, to cook, made all the difference in the world. It meant I could spend more time with the children, including have Daddy chats when necessary, and that was invaluable.

Those lasagnes represented exactly the sort of help I needed from the mothers in our area whom Emma had befriended over the years. What I didn't need – and yet regularly got – was having to listen to some mothers almost in tears on the phone to me, telling me how devastated they were by Emma's illness, how they couldn't stop thinking about her, and about all the good times together when they used to go to the park with the children, go to toddler groups, and chat over lovely cups of tea. Unbelievably, some people seemed to think it was appropriate to cry on my shoulder. Maybe they were trying to prove to me how close they were to Emma, or that they really empathised with me because they too were devastated. I don't know. As far as I am concerned, their grief was all about their own inability to deal with mortality and loss, and those people got deleted from my mental list of friends fairly quickly. Because the fact was, I didn't have time to analyse or rationalise other people's reactions. We were doing the 110 metre sprint hurdles – Emma's cancer was evolving fast and brutally, and its treatment was intense from the start – and I couldn't stop along the way to drag people over the hurdles with me, nor look over my shoulder and ask myself why these people weren't able to keep up and if I was offending them by running on ahead. This illness sets you apart from others who can act thoughtlessly, without meaning to. The result is that you feel alone and isolated because no one else seems to understand what you are going through.

Some so-called friends did not need me to delete them from any list. They deleted themselves. They made themselves scarce, and were of no practical or emotional help whatsoever. But none behaved with quite the same jaw-dropping egocentricity as the couple who turned up one morning when I happened to be outside the house. We considered them to be really good friends of ours with whom we had shared many a crazy guitar and singing session in the past, and summer barbecues that had flowed on into the early evening. But that day, they pulled up in their Volvo and, without bothering to get out of the car, the husband simply wound the window down and said to me, with barely a trace of concern or embarrassment in his voice that I could detect, 'Jon, really sorry, but we've decided to let you get on with it.' Other than nearly telling them to get lost there and then, I was left completely and utterly speechless. I mean, they had driven all the way over to the house, hadn't bothered to get out of the car, then delivered a line like that. That took some doing!

I looked at the husband and joked, 'Well, I suppose you'd better get on with whatever it is you're doing,' before turning round and walking back into the house. Again, I just didn't have the time or the energy to work out what on earth had possessed them and I was actually laughing as I went back up the stairs because it seemed so outrageous. The fact was, I had absolutely no idea what their reasons were because they hadn't taken the trouble to explain anything to me. If they'd at least got out of the car, asked after Emma, discussed the situation a bit, then told me that they found her illness very difficult to cope with 'because . . .' I might have understood. After all, maybe they'd been touched by cancer themselves and it brought back terrible memories, maybe they felt useless in this sort of situation, maybe even, as Scientologists, there was a more mysterious reason underneath those words. But no, inasmuch as I knew them, what they said and did was totally out of character, and I will never forget it.

Fairly early on, even when Emma was at home, the routine didn't vary much, because she would be in bed not long after the children. She was desperate to cling on to her role of being a mother to them, so she tried to be around when they came back from school, would read them bedtime stories in the evening, and even, on the odd occasion, stood outside the school gates in one of her many coloured headscarves to welcome them at the end of their day. She didn't care that people saw her like that, and she certainly wasn't going to hide herself away just because she had cancer. If people felt uncomfortable when they saw her, that was their problem, not hers. One of the things cancer patients crave is for others to treat them as the person they always were, and still are. Just because they are ill doesn't mean they have become a different person who no longer wants to be involved in everyday life.

She tried so hard to live normally, even though the treatment was clearly making her feel worse and worse; but increasingly, her way of asserting herself was to reproach me for letting her do some of the routine tasks around the house. 'You still made me fill the washing machine,' she would shout at me. 'Can't you see I'm tired? I can hardly walk, for God's sake!' 'Hang on a minute,' I wanted to reply, 'you said you wanted to do that, I'm trying to give you your dignity here, so get on with it and don't shout at me. If you don't want to do it, then fine. Because every day you're not here, I do it. So don't give me a bollocking.' But I would bite my lip and say nothing. On other occasions, she would criticise me for doing something wrong, or not like she used to do it. One morning, Sam had come down fully dressed before breakfast. 'I'm not hungry, Dad,' he had told me. 'I'm just going to brush my teeth.' And because I had allowed him to do that, she had crawled down the stairs in a fury simply because I hadn't forced him to eat something. 'You're hopeless, what a stupid thing to do, you know he shouldn't do that!' Emma was starting to lose her role, and she couldn't bear to see that happening. I knew it, and I could see how incredibly sad that made her and how incredibly difficult it was for her. And the way she expressed that sadness was to lash out at me.

But it was difficult for me, too: the children and I had our own routine now, it worked very well, and in a terrible way, having her come back every four days for 48 hours – if that –

was almost an inconvenience. Not because we didn't want her there. But because we had managed to adjust well to our new life, and had had to do so at very short notice, and whenever Emma came home, we were forced back into our 'before' life, except that it wasn't really our 'before' life, it was a sham version of it. I was in limbo: most of the time, I was living as a single parent, thinking that this was now going to be our life. Then Emma would come briefly back, throw us into turmoil again, and without intending to, would ratchet up the level of tension between us that was slowly but surely beginning to rise.

Most evenings, by the time the children were in bed, I was shattered. I would try to eat something, then get on with returning the backlog of phone calls that had accumulated during the day. People often phoned when it was not possible to talk to them, so I would have to promise to call them back. I could never just leave the phone to ring, because I would never know if it was maybe the hospital calling to say that Emma had gone neutrapenic, or, if she was at home, asking me to delay bringing her in the next day because there wasn't a bed for her.

One evening, when Emma was in hospital, and about a month into her treatment, I had just finished tidying the house after a normal hectic day, and had finally collapsed into bed with the intention of watching TV for a few minutes before falling asleep. I had barely been in bed for a minute when my heart sank: I realised that I had forgotten to feed the guinea pigs . . . and it was absolutely pouring with rain outside. We already had a cat, but the children had recently acquired two guinea pigs, which they decided to call Lucy and Emily. Goodness knows why they were given those names, because it gave the impression that they had personalities, whereas really they were just little guinea pigs whose only care in the world was a regular supply of straw and food. Still, I reasoned, they didn't deserve to go hungry. I knew I had no choice: I had to go back outside to feed them. Reluctantly, I got up, pulled on a pair of jeans, put on a raincoat and some flip flops because I was going to get my feet absolutely drenched anyway, and struggled out in the drilling rain.

I had just slumped back into bed, still soaking wet from my brief trip outside, when the phone rang. Cursing the interruption, I grabbed the receiver. It was Jo, one of Emma's closest friends. 'Hi, how are you, Jon?' she asked, probably taken aback at the gruff way I had answered the phone. 'The guinea pigs have got to go,' I shot back before I'd even properly said hello. Because that precise moment was when it hit me: life was never, ever going to be the same. This was going to be the practical, everyday reality of what my life was going to be. I had done a month of it, and whatever happened in the future, it wasn't going to get any easier. I was going to be on a treadmill, and there was no getting off. And quite simply, those guinea pigs had no place at all in that life. They did not fit into the routine, a routine that I now had to make as efficient as possible if I was going to survive. They were history, as far as I was concerned. The night with the guinea pigs was a huge turning point in how I viewed the future, and the next morning they were gone, back to the lady we had got them from. The kids, who had other things on their mind by then, barely noticed.

During the early weeks of Emma's treatment, my emotions fluctuated. After the diagnosis in Stanmore, I had almost been laughing when we had got back in the car, because finally, after weeks of waiting, we knew what we were facing, and to me that had felt almost surreal. But then, soon after, the shock of the diagnosis set in, not that I was aware of it at the time, and I only understood how deep that shock went, how far it embedded itself in my psyche, weeks and even years later. In fact, only now am I coming to realise that the matter-of-fact way in which I handled the situation at first was probably in part due to shock, because initially there were no tears. I just got on with it, and dealt with whatever had to be dealt with. Nor was there ever any lamenting, any 'why her?' or 'it's so unfair'. Indeed, there never has been. That is not in my make-up and it seems utterly pointless to question why something as horrific as this happens. The fact is it does, and randomly so, and it makes no sense to torture oneself by trying to find out why.

For her part, Emma never spoke to me about the possibility of dying, and it was clear to me from the outset that she was absolutely determined to get going with the treatment as soon as possible, to have any operation or operations required, and to rid her body of this cancer. The reason she was prepared to go through this terrible treatment was that it would make her better. There was never any other scenario in her mind: she wanted to live, and she was going to live. As a result, we never discussed what might happen if the treatment didn't work, we never speculated about hypothetical scenarios, we never looked further than the next dose of chemo. And my role was to stay strong for her, because the alternative was simply not an option. Emma herself was an immensely strong person, but the only time she would start to falter or worry was if she saw that I was anxious about something. So I knew that, in order for her to stay psychologically resilient and to be able to cope with the physical and mental trial that she was now facing, I had to give her what she needed from me. And that did not mean discussing her future in terms of the bleakest of outcomes, or revealing my doubts or fears; rather, it meant being unshakably strong for her and the children, and acknowledging the benefits of the treatment.

Before Emma started her treatment, I began asking questions about myself. I knew my wife was going to die, and I knew that it was going to be horrible for her. But what nobody was able to tell me was what was I going to experience? What could I expect? I had no idea, no understanding of what was going to happen to me emotionally both during her illness and, importantly, after. Yes, I knew that in practical terms I was going to have to look after Emma, the kids, the house, and that was all fine. But no one was able to tell me how extraordinarily deeply this would affect me, because everyone who has lived through a similar situation and such an immense loss reacts differently. That said, while I did end up talking briefly to a bereavement counsellor as well as a child psychologist attached to the Macmillan Unit, I never wanted to rely on the many bereavement or cancer services available because I thought the counsellors did not really know and understand me as a person, or know our particular circumstances. I'm sure they help many people, and I am genuinely glad they do, but on the whole I needed to work through the issues by myself. I needed to go through the process on my own, and, as long as I had the support of close friends of mine when I needed it, I knew I could cope.

As well as being very unsure about what awaited me emotionally, within a few weeks I reached a stage where my abiding emotion was one of profound, intense sadness. That autumn, when Emma was in hospital for most of the time, was when I truly started to grieve for her and for the life we had once had. And I grieved for her in such a way that there was hardly a second in the day when I didn't know that I was slowly losing my wife, the woman whom I truly considered to be my other half and the one whom I had always imagined would accompany me through life for many years to come. The intensity of the emotion was sometimes so shockingly great that it threatened to overwhelm me. And the realisation that there was no way of avoiding it, that I had to live through this nightmare, that no one could do it for me, no one could make it any better or make it go away, shook me right down to my inner core. Sometimes, I would go to sleep exhausted, then wake early the next morning literally shaking like a leaf, having had no respite in my sleep from my daytime nightmare, from constantly thinking of what would happen to the children, to Emma, and afterwards when she was no longer there. Usually, I am emotionally tough when I need to be. I know that, and I can cope with an awful lot of things, but I did sometimes wonder during those autumn months how I was ever going to cope.

As the nights drew in, the leaves fell off the trees and the bleakness of winter approached, I went through some dark, dark, times. Once the children were safely in bed, I often used to sit at the kitchen table, and that is when I did my thinking, my grieving, and my crying. That is when I began, very slowly, to accept that I was going to have to let go of Emma. I would often sit there with a bottle of wine and my guitar, singing songs to myself, Neil Young songs such as 'Like a Hurricane', which somehow seemed to touch a particularly raw nerve. Some of these songs I had sung for years, others I had long wanted to teach myself, but all of them took on an extraordinarily powerful meaning. The one that affected me the most, and the one I still cannot listen to because the lyrics affect me too much, even though it's on my iPod, is 'I Believe in You'.

Those evenings spent sitting at the kitchen table during the last few months of 2003 were the bleakest. While Emma was in hospital, that was when I would get really, really upset and shed untold amounts of tears as I tried to come to terms that it was over, our relationship was going to end, and Emma was going to die.

Friends did what they could, and two of my close friends in particular, Pete and Mike, guys I had known for 20 years, were fantastic. They would ring up and ask how I was. 'I feel like shit,' I would freely admit to them, and they would just let me talk. They didn't try to offer advice, or tell me, as others sometimes did, that they could imagine how awful I felt – how could they? They had never been through what I was going through. Anyway, Mike and Pete knew those sorts of comments would have grated on me. One evening, I was feeling particularly low when the phone rang. It was Mike. When he realised quite how bad I was, he didn't hesitate. 'Right, I'm coming over. I'll bring a couple of beers and we'll talk.'

'Don't be stupid, Mike, it's 10 o'clock. It's fine. Really.'

'No, I'll see you in a minute,' and he put the phone down.

He lives in Hampton Court, which is hardly next door, but as far as he was concerned, there was no question in his mind: he had to come over. He turned up almost an hour later clutching two bottles of very horrible beer and we sat there talking late into the night. And I will never forget that he was willing to drop everything, get in the car and drive over, just so that I had somebody to talk to during my darkest moments.

For the first two months of Emma's treatment, I still had to go off every two weeks to the Grand Prix races, to honour my commitment to Ferrari. Whenever I went away, we had to make sure that Emma's parents could come over to look after the children, and that friends were also able to step in whenever necessary. Many of them had commitments and busy lives, and working out who could look after the kids on which days required a lot of forward planning and organisation. But we were lucky in that we discovered enough true friends who unhesitatingly helped us out with the practicalities of looking after the children.

At the end of September, however, I had to go away for two whole weeks, which was the longest I had been away since Emma had been diagnosed. First, I had to go to the Indianapolis Grand Prix, then to Los Angeles to do some pictures for Olympus, on to Japan to do more work for them, and finally on to the final race of my season in mid-October in Suzuka. Although it was a long time for me to be away, Emma was still in the relatively early days of her treatment and so wasn't as ill as she soon would be. A month later, and the trip would not have been possible, which is why I didn't go to Brazil for the final race of the season. As it was, it did me good to get away. As with the Rolling Stones concert, I needed to take a break from the relentless strain of what was going on at home. I needed to be amongst people who did not know that my wife had cancer, and who treated me in a completely normal way, rather than tip-toeing around me as if I was fragile and about to break. I needed to keep working not only financially, of course, but also because of my sanity. And I know some people found that difficult to understand. Some 'friends' found it distasteful that I should go away at this time, and leave my sick wife behind. But all I will say to those people who judged, and who doubted my ability to look after my wife and my children as a result of the choices I made at the time, is that if they ever go through a similar situation, God forbid, they will understand why I did those things. And they will also realise that when it comes to this illness, you can never judge others for what they do and don't do. I know that it helped me to go away, Emma was in total agreement, and I absolutely do not regret my decision.

The other unexpected benefit of going away was that it was during that trip that I finally found the most useful source of information on osteosarcoma. It was actually the website of a specialist cancer hospital in Indianapolis which is part of the Indiana University School of Medicine and is one of the largest units of its kind in the world. Ironically, in the way life sometimes has of bringing together seemingly unrelated parts of our existence, I had driven past this enormous hospital every day on my way to the track at Indianapolis. The many buildings, which stretch all the way down several blocks, struck me at the time as having an air of impressive efficiency and superiority. I decided that the people who worked there must surely know something about osteosarcoma, so I emailed them, via the 'Contact Us' tab on their website. They very quickly answered and said that although they couldn't give me advice about a specific case, they were directing me to a number of articles from their research archives. That was exactly what I needed: practical information, hard, medically sound facts, and answers to some of my questions. I wasn't searching for a glimmer of hope, so it wasn't a blow for me to read the material. Rather, it provided some vital, missing pieces of the puzzle of what the illness actually entailed.

I immediately got confirmation that Emma's prognosis was, as I knew, extremely poor. She had high-grade central osteosarcoma (because it was in the middle of the bone), which had already metastasised to the lungs, the normal course of progression for this type of tumour, and showed that it was already advanced. It was indeed a childhood cancer, as we had been told, affecting adolescents in particular when bone growth suddenly turns cancerous. The long bones in the arms and legs are usually affected and 80 per cent of osteosarcomas develop in the bones around the knee, either in the lower part of the thigh bone, or femur, where Emma's had developed, or in the upper part of the tibia, the lower leg bone. There was now no doubt in my mind that, whatever treatment the doctors attempted, it would not ultimately affect the long-term outcome.

It was not for the doctors to tell Emma this, especially as she had not asked. Doctors are very skilled at 'reading' the patient and divulging only as much necessary information as the patient seems able to cope with – and to want. It was clear when we had seen Stephen Cannon in Stanmore that Emma wanted to be treated, that she felt she could beat this illness, and that she desperately wanted to live. So we were not going to have any discussions with doctors that did not entail helping Emma to reach her goal. And I was not going to have any discussions with her concerning anything I might or might not have found out on the Internet. As far as she was concerned, she trusted her team of doctors absolutely (as she was right to do), they were going to do whatever was needed and she was going to survive. End of story. No need for further research, no need for further questions.

I, on the other hand, would return to the Indianapolis website at each stage of Emma's illness and would contact them directly to obtain from them the answers to questions that I was not able to ask her doctors. Not because they didn't know the answers themselves, but because I was not their patient, and I was not able to have one-to-one time with them to ask them the many difficult questions I really wanted to. The information I received from Indianapolis was invaluable and showed me how crucial it was for me to arm myself with the facts. It was essential for me that I knew in advance what was likely to happen, even if I didn't know exactly when, so that I could anticipate each battle before it began. After all, what was the alternative? The alternative, I felt, was to be uninformed, to have a 'wait and see' attitude, to believe naively that everything would be okay, and to be caught unawares when the cancerous cells that were now freely circulating throughout Emma's body finally started winning the war. That would then leave me totally unprepared and ill equipped to help Emma and the children, and that was a completely unacceptable scenario. I believed that the only thing to do was to be pragmatic, realistic and to be as informed as possible. In short, I had to know the truth.

7

The Christmas Casualty

WHILST EMMA WAS being brutalised by the chemotherapy, and I was having to accept the stark reality of her condition, her parents were having to cope with a vicious truth of their own: their youngest child, their only daughter, had cancer and might not survive. For Emma's parents to have to face that prospect must have been unimaginable and appalling, which is maybe why they never asked me outright what their daughter's prognosis was. They would call me to ask how a hospital appointment had gone, what the doctors had said, or how Emma was that day, but they never discussed their fears with me, nor asked me questions that might require comfortless answers. I don't know what they knew or what they had worked out for themselves, although I suspect they feared the worst from early on. But I didn't feel it was my job to call them to confirm that their daughter was indeed going to die. As it turned out, it was a full three years after her death that I revealed I had known all along that Emma's illness was terminal. Although they were shocked to learn this, they made it clear that in no way did they resent me for withholding the truth of the situation from them. I had done so because to have told them at the time would have utterly destroyed them, and it would have been grossly unfair to inflict such agony on them. My relationship with them, furthermore,

was different from a father–son relationship or the one I had
with my own children. And whilst I remain angry at not being
told about my father's illness until almost the very end, and
whilst this shaped my resolve to be open with my own children
about their mother's illness, I don't feel my relationship with
Emma's parents was such that I had to inflict information on
them that they hadn't requested. Had they enquired, clearly that
would have been different. And when they did ask me certain
questions, naturally I would answer them, but I didn't tell them
any more than they seemed to want to know. Emma's illness
was, I am sure, overwhelmingly terrifying and devastating for
them, and they must have lived through many months of hell,
and their way of coping with it was to throw themselves into
helping her as much as possible. If they had been told the truth,
as I had been, they might have found it even more painful than
it already was to help and support their daughter. And it was vital
for Emma that those around her were strong and believed in her
ability to survive so that she in turn could maintain her own
strength and tenacity.

Once the Grand Prix season was over, in mid-October, I had
one final job to complete – a travel story at the end of October
involving a trip to an exotic island off the coast of Thailand.
After that, I would be ceasing all work until the start of the new
Formula 1 season the following March. When I left, Emma was
in hospital, so her parents came over to look after the children
for the five days that I was away. I had hoped the job would be
stress free. After all, I was staying in a luxury hotel on the edge
of a palm-fringed beach. In normal circumstances, this would
have been a gift of an assignment, a glamorous bonus to round
off a hectic season. But the idyllic setting almost went out of its

way to serve as a complete contrast to the misery, fear and confusion that was gripping Emma back home.

Emma had now been having chemo for around eight weeks, and because she had reacted so well, she was in a position where an operation to remove the primary tumour in her knee was looking likely. The issue was when. The debate centred around whether she should continue a bit longer with the chemo, or whether she should stop it for a short while in order to regain a bit of strength before the operation, or even whether she should continue with the chemo right up until the operation, then be more or less wheeled straight into theatre. She was desperate to have the surgery, but was also desperate to continue with the chemo as long as possible. Meanwhile, Jeremy Whelan and his team at the Middlesex were liaising with Stephen Cannon in Stanmore who would be performing the actual operation. They were hesitating about its timing because they were unsure that Emma was strong enough to undergo such a major procedure. The fact was, there was a possibility that she might actually die on the operating table. Emma was so frustrated by the lack of concrete information that she bombarded me with anxious phone calls during the entire time that I was in Thailand, and begged me to speak to the doctors to find out what was going on. 'I don't know what I'm doing,' she kept repeating, increasingly frantically. 'I can't get hold of these people; they won't tell me what's going on.' So I would try to speak to them myself, even though most of the time, I would only manage to get hold of the doctors' secretaries. 'Oh, Jeremy will be doing his rounds later on, he's not available right now,' they would say. I'm sure it was true, but I too started to feel very frustrated, not helped by the physical distance there was between me and the hospital. 'Listen,' I ended up screaming down the phone to them one day, 'I'm calling you from Thailand. It's midnight here, can somebody *please* go and speak to my wife!'

By the time I flew back to England, Emma had had another neutrapenic episode and had been rushed to Guildford's Royal Surrey hospital. I finally arrived home at seven o'clock in the morning, after an interminable 12-hour flight, to be met outside the house by Emma's mum. I was even more tense and exhausted than when I had left. 'So, what are you going to do now?' she asked, with evident strain in her voice.

'Well, I'm going to have a shower, I'm going to get the kids to school, then I'm going to grab a couple of hours' sleep,' I replied as evenly as I could.

At that, and in a way that was totally out of character, she exploded. 'How dare you, how dare you! Why aren't you going to the hospital to see your wife!'

I was completely taken aback, I had never seen her like this, but I realised at that moment that she obviously had a very clear opinion of what she thought I should be doing, and it clearly didn't tally with mine. 'She's my wife,' I said firmly.

'But she's my daughter,' she replied, sobbing. 'You don't know what it's like!'

That was when I had to explain to her something that I felt very strongly about: I was Emma's next of kin and my decisions about her were not going to be governed by her mother. It was vital that she understood that, however difficult it undoubtedly was for her. I imagine part of her deep sadness came from the terrible realisation that she was not going to be the one making the decisions about her daughter's life or what remained of it, and, although it gave me no pleasure to do so, I had been forced to clarify the situation, because otherwise the issue would have arisen over and over again. Emma's mum must have accepted what I said, because after that outburst there were never any further problems between us. But it was another indication that cancer does things to people and their relationships, that it can lead to terrible things being said, some of which are never forgotten and sometimes, even, never forgiven. And no one warns you about this in advance.

I tried, and mostly failed, through anger, to get a bit of sleep, then duly went in to see Emma later that morning. I found her in an isolation room, hooked up to an antibiotic drip, looking very pale. What shocked me the most, though, was the state of the room: there was dust on the floor, the loo and bathroom were filthy, there was hair everywhere, and the paper cups that had been used to take medicines littered the floor. What was more, the nurses on the ward couldn't speak English. I was fuming and berated them for the dirty rooms before realising that it was a pointless exercise. Instead, I started striding up and down the corridor opening various doors until I found the cupboard where they kept the cleaning products. I grabbed a broom and some disinfectant and started to clean my wife's room, something I would not expect anyone in our situation to have to do. Fortunately, despite everything, Emma fought off the fever, and recovered sufficiently to allow the oncology team to schedule the longed-for knee operation in Stanmore as soon as a suitable slot arose.

For Emma, this was fantastic news, because she felt that once she had the primary tumour removed, she could finish her chemotherapy, have the secondary tumours removed from her lungs with two further operations – one on each lung – and she would then be cancer free. On more than one occasion, in the lead-up to the knee operation, we discussed the lung tumours with Jeremy Whelan and he would always emphasise, as if he was anticipating our next question, 'I'm not going to tell you how many there are, because it's irrelevant. That fact is, you've got some tumours, but don't worry about it. The main thing is to get through your chemo. Once you have had your knee operation, we'll discuss it then.' For him, it was very much a question of one step at a time.

Emma was finally admitted to Stanmore about a month before Christmas. By then, she had spent barely a few days at home over the previous few weeks, either because she hadn't been strong enough to leave the Middlesex for the full two days in between her four-day cycles of chemo, or because she had gone neutrapenic as soon as she got home, and had had to go into the Royal Surrey to recover. Her body was getting weaker and weaker, and when I drove her up for the operation on a dark, grey December morning, she was not in good shape, and was very, very tired. She was also extremely nervous and scared. When Stephen Cannon saw her, it had been over three months since that blazingly hot August day when he had said, 'And I'm not sure I can treat you,' and he admitted he was shocked to be operating on her. He was surprised that she had got to this stage, not because he thought she would be dead by now (he wasn't that tactless or explicit!), but because he didn't think there would have been a sufficient reaction to the chemo to warrant his subsequent intervention. Ironically, of course, this encouraged Emma to think she really was making great strides in her bid to fight off this illness, but Stephen Cannon did also make clear, as he had done back in August, that there was still every chance – greater than 50/50, as he put it – that, in the process of removing the tumour, he would discover that it had invaded the surrounding tissue, muscles, ligaments and tendons so much that he would be forced to amputate her leg.

Knowing that this was a distinct possibility, I had already done some Internet research about artificial limbs in order to keep one step ahead of potential developments. So I spent a long time reading up on the company in Dorset that supplies Heather Mills with all those incredibly realistic legs. I knew that, should Emma lose her leg, the implications for her in terms of the sheer practicalities of everyday life would be extreme. Although I knew Emma needed a complete miracle to survive her particular cancer – and I didn't believe in miracles – I thought at this stage that she might have maybe a year or 15 months left, thanks to the barbaric treatment that she was willingly putting herself through. The idea that she would not be able to drive a car during that time, that she would lose what little independence she still had, was horrifying for me. It probably was to her as well but, as ever, we did not discuss the 'what if?' scenario. What was the point in speculating? We would discuss it only if it reached that stage.

As they wheeled Emma down to theatre, I stayed with her all the way. She was clutching my hand and, when she looked at me, her eyes revealed a level of fear that I had never seen before, despite everything she had already been through over the last few months. I had never seen Emma look that terrified and I was utterly powerless to do anything about it. All I could say to her was, 'Don't worry, be calm. These guys know what they're doing. I'll be there when you come out.' But holding on to Emma's hand tightly just before she was anaesthetised, looking down at my wife, and wondering whether she would be waking up as an amputee, was one of the three or four defining times during her illness when I just felt desperately sad and sorry for her.

The operation itself lasted seven and a half hours. The tumour – which I subsequently discovered was an enormous 8 x 6 x 5cm mass – was protruding from the femur like a huge tear drop, and was coming out of the back of the knee. Stephen Cannon had said to her that he didn't know exactly what would happen during the operation, because he would go in, have a look around, then take it from there. Meanwhile, I was told that the operation would take at least five hours, so I settled into the waiting area with yet more 'Hospital Copy' issues of *Good Housekeeping* magazine, circa 1982. I had some music to listen to, a TV was on in the corner of the room, and I had the day's papers to leaf through. Even then, time entered another dimension of slowness. Every now and again, I would dash off to get myself some brown liquid, passing itself off as coffee, from a vending machine. Occasionally, a nurse would emerge to give me news of progress. 'She's still in there, but everything is going fine.' Of course, that meant everything and nothing, but at least it was news of sorts. Five hours came and went, and still no sign of the end of the operation. Six hours, seven hours. Time ticked on. It was dark outside when the nurse finally came to tell me that Emma was out of theatre, and in the recovery room. And yes, Stephen Cannon had managed to save her leg. Relief and deep gratitude for the brilliance of the surgeon and the medical team flooded through me.

I went to see Emma as soon as I was allowed to. By then, she had been taken straight to intensive care and was surrounded by tubes and bleeping machines. A nurse sat permanently at the foot of her bed, checking her blood levels, her blood pressure, her heartbeat, and all the other vital signs that would alert the medical staff if anything started to go catastrophically wrong. Even in a stronger person, the sort of operation Emma had endured counted as major surgery. Given the state she was in, it was nothing short of extraordinary that she had survived it so well. Mr Cannon had removed a huge part of both the femur and the tibia, below the knee, and replaced them with huge metal rods that would now need to take on the role of the missing bone. Emma's leg was lying beneath a protective metal frame, and it now had a scar that ran from halfway down her shin almost all the way up to her hip.

If I was being honest, I had had severe misgivings about whether it was worth doing this operation, given how risky it was, and that it was not going to change the eventual outcome. Resources and time were clearly scarce at the hospital and in cancer care in general, so I thought the hospital might be better off operating on someone – a child, maybe – who genuinely had some chance of survival, rather than on Emma. On the other hand, for Emma to have the tumour removed was essential for her mental well-being. She had longed for this operation because it represented a major step towards a full recovery. She would now feel that she was one step – and a big one, at that – closer to a cure. And I couldn't deny her that hope.

She took a long time to start emerging from the anaesthetic, but the first thing I said to her when she started coming round was, 'You didn't lose your leg.' There was no reaction but I hoped she had heard me. And I hoped she would now be less frightened.

Although Emma would be in hospital for a while, within 48 hours she was out of intensive care. A few days later, she even sat up in bed and announced, 'God, I feel good!' as if she had simply had a wonderfully long and restorative sleep. Maybe that was down to the major blood transfusion, which had temporarily buoyed her up, or maybe she felt relief because the root cause of her cancer was no longer inside her. Either way, she was determined to get out as quickly as possible so that she could continue with the chemo. She was soon out of bed, pushing herself through the long, painful sessions of physiotherapy, putting increasing pressure on her leg, and doing everything she possibly could to speed the healing process.

Meanwhile, a friend of mine at the BBC had got us tickets and behind-the-scenes passes for the children and me to go and watch *Top of the Pops* in the studio, so I decided that we would go to the recording of the show, which took place at the BBC in White City and lasted about three hours, then go on to Stanmore to enable the children to visit their mother whom they hadn't seen for a couple of weeks. We would also spend the night in a hotel nearby which had a pool, because it was too far to drive back to Haslemere after what would inevitably be a long day. The idea was to make a bit of a weekend of it, and to make the trip as enjoyable as possible. The *Top of the Pops* bit was great and the kids loved meeting Fearne Cotton, and Kelly Osbourne who walked in and promptly started swearing like a trooper until she spotted the children on the sofa and came over to apologise – which they thought was fantastic, of course.

After the show, we left for the hospital. That was the point when what had been a fun day out turned into the day from hell, when a journey which should have taken us an hour, at most, took nearly three. We could have run it in less. The traffic was appalling and by the time we arrived at the hospital, after checking into what turned out to be a gruesome motel-like hotel, I was exhausted and it was nearly six o'clock. The children were ecstatic to see their mother again and spent much of the time cuddling her and filling her in on every detail of their trip to the studios. Emma too was elated at seeing her children again and the fact that she hadn't been able to accompany them on their trip was of no consequence to her, because even in normal times, she would not have done so. The tickets had been through a friend of mine, so the trip would have fallen in the category of 'a day out with Dad', rather than yet another occasion that her illness had forced her to miss out on. Anyway, she was so glad to see her children that she was hardly going to begrudge them their happiness. To add to the merry mood, the nurses made a huge fuss of the children, cooing over how wonderful they were. In contrast, I sat slumped in a chair nearby, desperate to get home. I was so drained of energy that, at that moment, I just wanted someone to pick me up and parachute me into my bed.

Within a couple of weeks, Emma was well enough to leave, but rather than go home to continue her recovery, she went straight back into the Middlesex for another dose of chemo because she wanted to catch up on the time she had lost while she had been in Stanmore. In her mind, it was still very much a case of 'the tumours are still in there, and until there is nothing left to cut out or to blast with drugs, the doctors haven't finished their work. So do what you have to do to me, because otherwise this thing is going to kill me. And I'm not dying.' Her ferocious instinct of survival had not been dimmed over the previous weeks. If anything, having survived the leg operation so well, she seemed even more convinced that she would eventually get the better of the cancer. And who was I to disillusion her?

She finally came home shortly before Christmas. Her leg was in a brace, she could only hobble around with difficulty, and she had to drag herself up and down the stairs on her backside, refusing all my offers of help out of pride. Despite her extra-ordinary determination, she was clearly very tired and fragile, both physically and mentally. The chemo had resulted in her losing weight. She was taking pills to counter the effects of nausea caused by the drugs, but they didn't always stop her from being sick. So she ate whenever she could, because there were times when she simply could not stomach the thought of any food, or when the mouth ulcers which were developing more and more as a result of her almost non-existent immune system made it too painful for her to swallow. In those instances, she would force herself to have one of the high-protein drinks that the hospital had given her, because she knew that if her weight dropped below a certain threshold, the chemo would have to stop.

The children had just broken up for Christmas and were incredibly happy to have their mum back for a few days, the longest she had actually been at home for about six weeks. But it was far from easy for them, because Emma spent most of the time in bed, especially at first, so they weren't able to spend as much time with her as they would have wanted. And when they did, she grew tired very easily, so was limited in what she could do with them. Nonetheless, for the first time in weeks, their mother was under the same roof as them and, what was more, we were actually going to be spending Christmas as a family.

One afternoon, soon after she had come home, Emma was upstairs in bed, and had called down to me, asking if I could make her a cup of tea. I had promptly put the kettle on. On cue, because children always have the knack of diverting your attention just when you have started doing something, I had to go into the living room where the kids were playing. They had inevitably started to argue over who was winning and who was cheating – the usual sibling disagreements. When I went back into the kitchen a few minutes later, I almost stopped in my tracks. Emma had obviously had enough of waiting. Annoyed that I couldn't even bring her a cup of tea when she wanted one, she had hauled herself out of bed, come down the stairs on her backside and had now appeared in the doorway. Before I could say anything, she rolled over on to her front and, silently, literally dragged herself, using her arms, across the kitchen floor. It was like watching a man climbing the last 100 metres of Everest with no oxygen. She was almost gasping with the sheer aching effort of it. I was appalled. This was as low as a human being could get. I was witnessing the defamation of life, the unbearable results of drugs which are so poisonous that they turn people into barely functioning human beings. I could not imagine inflicting greater cruelty on someone than that which Emma was currently enduring. This was my wife, the woman whose beauty and personality had knocked me out from the very first time I had set eyes on her, and who was now reduced to the level of a wounded, dying animal, crawling across a field in desperate search of safety or shelter. The difference was that, if she really had been a wounded animal, I would have shot her out of compassion in order to spare her further suffering, whereas as a person her torment was relentless. I would have ended her life for her, there and then, shocking as that might seem to someone who has not experienced what I was going through at that moment. But that is how inhuman Emma's situation was.

I said nothing when I first saw her. And I did not immediately rush over to pick her up, because I knew I would be verbally attacked if I did. Pride was going to get her across the kitchen floor, as well as her utter desperation to survive, and to have intervened would have meant total humiliation for her. I could not stand there for long, though, and as soon as she reached the table, I helped her into a chair without saying a word, and carried on making the delayed cup of tea. It was another instance, though, when intense, deep, sadness for Emma flooded through me. I had seen the sheer terror in her eyes just before she had had her knee operation. Now I had seen her on all fours, stripped of all dignity yet wanting to cling on to some vestige of normality by proving that she was still able to make a cup of tea. And both times, I had felt bitterly, profoundly sorry for her.

Later that evening, as I sat alone downstairs, reflecting on what I had seen earlier that day, I did seriously question how much more I was going to be able to take. The sheer unremitting awfulness of the situation meant that, from then on, that thought never left me for long. Whenever I was driving, whenever I was alone at night, when I was out chopping logs for the fire, or simply watching the children play, I often used to think, 'How much more do I have to take, because I don't think I can take it for much longer. If you're going to die, do it! Die!'

I wanted to make Christmas special, so, with the children, we had decorated an enormous tree before Emma had got home. It was looking beautiful and magical, and, on Christmas morning, there was a mound of sparkly, multicoloured parcels around it that made it look like a picture-perfect scene. The children tore excitedly at the wrapping paper and squealed with happiness as they frenziedly opened up their presents. Before long, they had scampered off with their booty and were settling down to work their way through it, trying out first one present, then another, before jumping on to a third. They were beside themselves with happiness, and it was comforting to see.

It was time for me to start preparing the Christmas lunch. I had planned the whole thing, and we were going to have the works: turkey, crispy roast potatoes, all the trimmings, followed by a steaming hot Christmas pudding. Later that morning, with the turkey browning in the oven, and the potatoes starting to crunch up nicely, I started to peel the carrots. Halfway through, I had to go next door to help Sam put together one of his new presents. I must have been gone two minutes, but by the time I went back into the kitchen, Emma was standing there by the cooker, hobbling around because of her brace, but chopping away at the vegetables with fierce resolve. When I saw her there was no doubt in my mind that she absolutely wanted to be doing this. For her, preparing the family Christmas lunch was what she was aching to do, and it would have been catastrophic for me to intervene. So I let her finish off the preparations. In fact, I thought it was great that she felt well enough to take over. Symbolically it gave her back a bit of her role of being the carer and provider, the mother who could feed her children. I thought it was important that she was able to claw back some of that role, even if it was only for the day. I was letting her have her life back a bit. And if she was tired afterwards, I reasoned, it didn't matter. She could fall asleep on the sofa during *The Wizard of Oz*.

She finished preparing the lunch, she didn't fall over in the process, we all ate far too much, and had a wonderful family Christmas. For the kids, especially, that was great. In the early evening, Emma went off to bed, as did the children, whilst I stayed up watching yet another *Only Fools and Horses* Christmas Special – or something similarly easy on the brain.

As I crept into bed, thinking Emma was asleep, she suddenly mumbled to me in the dark, 'I can't believe you even made me cook the Christmas lunch.' I was completely stunned. The tone was unmistakeable: nasty, resentful, and full of hatred. Or that's what it sounded like to me. It was as if she had winded me in the stomach. I was horrified, and my immediate reaction was that I felt like punching her. That was all I wanted to do. I was fuming, livid, and simply could not believe my ears. How dare she! All I had done, I thought, was try to give her back some dignity, some sense of still belonging in the house, of still having a role, of not being a reduced, pathetic shell of the person she had once been. If I had said to her, when she had been at the stove, 'Oh, don't do that, go and sit down,' she would no doubt have insisted, 'No, it's fine, I'll just finish doing this.' Here I was, I felt, having bust my arse to get Christmas organised, having bought the presents, done the shopping and most of the cooking, having in effect done what many mothers and wives do every year. And now, because I had let her take over a small part of the 'show', she had turned round and kicked me in the teeth, as if I had forced her to slave all day over the hot stove like an old-fashioned, inconsiderate, unreconstructed male would have done, when in reality, nothing could have been further from the truth because I was happy to do all the work, and had been doing it without any problems for many weeks.

There was absolutely no point in responding to her words. I swallowed my anger, sighed heavily to indicate that I was nonetheless annoyed with her, turned over and tried to get to sleep. And the next day, we didn't discuss the matter further because I knew what the problem was: despite the happiness of being reunited as a family for Christmas, this was a really difficult time for Emma and me. She was feeling very unwell indeed, and uncomfortable that the roles within our relationship were changing. I had lost count of the number of times when one or other of the children had asked for something, whether it was a sticking plaster because they had cut themselves, or some paper to draw on. Whereas in the past, they would automatically have run to their mother, now they were starting their sentence with 'Dad, can I have . . .' even if she was in the same room as them. That must have cut straight to the quick for Emma. And it was horrible for me too, because I knew how much that hurt her. The only weapon she had to counter the pain was to nitpick at what I did, criticise me and undermine whatever I did if it wasn't exactly as she would have done it. My job was not to answer back, to be subservient to her emotions, and to let her vent her frustration, but that in turn caused increasing tension between us.

We never argued over the issue, and I wasn't asking for her gratitude that I was managing to run the house and look after the children reasonably well. As it was, she felt guilty about what she was putting us through, and she had said in the past that it was all her fault. 'What do you mean, how can it be your fault? You've done nothing wrong!' I had tried to reassure her. But I knew that, deep down, they were empty words because nothing I would say would convince her of the contrary. So I wasn't asking her – or anyone else, for that matter – to pat me on the back every day. Nor did I want to stretch out my arms in front of her and go, 'Oh, poor me, poor me.' But just once, just once, instead of the constant snide digs that she now directed at me, I would have liked her to say, 'Jon, I love you so much, and you're doing such a great job. Thank you.' But she never did. Ever. And that hurt me.

The fact is, just because someone has cancer, that doesn't mean their partner doesn't have feelings, and doesn't suffer about the way their relationship is going. And that's what was happening to me. Clearly I cared that our relationship was deteriorating because of the illness, but I wasn't going to say to Emma, 'Hey, we need to sit down and discuss where our relationship is going,' because that would have opened up a vast sea of additional issues, not least whether her illness meant we even had a future together. I didn't want to have that conversation because I knew I had a different view from Emma about what lay ahead; as a result, we both left things unsaid about what was happening to us. Yes, that may have increased the tension between us but, in hindsight, would I have done things differently and embarked on an analysis of our relationship? No. That would have been inappropriate. Emma had enough to handle without heaping another set of problems on her.

The following evening, Emma was curled up on the sofa watching *Casualty* with the children. They loved the programme and not even Emma's illness could dampen their passion for it. On the contrary, the children were now displaying precocious knowledge of medical terminology, which helped them to appreciate even more the key moments of tension in the programme. This week, it so happened that one of the plot lines involved a cancer patient. Neither the children nor Emma seemed fazed by this, and carried on watching happily enough. I was only half watching by this stage. At one point, the doctor had to tell the wife that her husband had lung cancer and was going to die. Sam, who was playing on the floor at Emma's feet, didn't even look up. 'He's got cancer,' he announced. 'Just like you, mummy. And he's going to die,' he carried on, oblivious, 'just like you.'

Emma looked at me, without batting an eyelid. She said nothing, and neither did I. I just walked out of the room, thinking, 'Shit, where did that come from?!' To this day, I'm still not sure how to explain Sam's comments, but once again, this little boy had spoken from somewhere deep within, somewhere that can only be reached by the subconscious and by instinct. And he was showing us adults just how extraordinary he was, and how much was going on inside his mind, without him even being aware of it.

8

Down the King's Road

EMMA STARTED CHEMOTHERAPY again a few days after Christmas. Within a couple of weeks, its toxic effects were once more ripping through her body and, what was most worrying, her knee started to show signs of infection. The two-foot-long scar had become red all around the knee area and Emma was developing a temperature, neither of which were good signs. The Royal Surrey's A&E department gave her some strong antibiotics – which delayed her next dose of chemo – but the concern was that her body might be starting to reject the many metal rods and pins inside her. Unfortunately, Emma was slow to react to the antibiotics, which wasn't surprising, given the amount she had already taken over the previous few months, so there was the serious possibility that the next stage would be to open her knee up again, clean it, sew it back up and hope that it didn't become re-infected. If it did, she might well have to lose her leg. That would have been a devastating blow to her, a first and real sign of defeat and, coming in the middle of the aggressive chemotherapy treatment she was still receiving, I feared for her mental health if her leg had to be amputated. I am far from sure that she would have survived the setback.

The problem with her knee lasted almost two months, during which time Emma's immune system and general health became immensely fragile. Her mouth ulcers got so bad that on one occasion she couldn't even open her mouth, because it had become one giant sore and her tongue looked like decomposing flesh. The ulcers weren't just in her mouth. They were all the way down her throat and oesophagus, so whenever she tried to eat or drink anything, which she still forced herself to do, she was in immense pain.

The medical staff were very helpful in advising us what Emma could do to ease some of her symptoms – certain vitamins were good for boosting the immune system, though high doses of vitamin C were contraindicated with chemotherapy. We also tried homeopathic remedies, which appeared to help a bit. Inevitably, I also researched on the Internet some of the more outlandish claims for curing cancer, or for helping with its symptoms. But I never thought they were the answer, in part because it seemed all the alternative or complementary methods needed the patient to start them *before* they tried the traditional, orthodox treatments, in particular chemotherapy. I believed, as did Emma, that we were with the one man who could make a difference and we would never have risked taking time out from whatever treatment Jeremy Whelan was offering. As for taking part in some last-ditch medical trial, which some people try to do in desperation, that presupposes the patient is even aware that it's a last throw of the dice, and that was not the case for Emma. So I didn't see the point in researching whether some hospital, somewhere in the world, might be trying some new 'wonder' drug which might extend her life by a few months, because that would also mean she would have to live far away from home for all that time which would simply not have been possible. Anyway, I knew, even if Emma didn't, that in all honesty nothing was going to make a permanent difference.

Some people have wondered why I didn't say more to Emma about her prognosis, or whether Emma might have known more about her situation than she was letting on. The fact of the matter is that I couldn't bear to lie to her; whatever way I looked at it, everything I had been told or had read online meant I could see no hope in the long term, and I felt that telling her the truth was just as bad for Emma's state of mind as offering her false hope. The fact was, I did know more about her cancer than Emma did – she didn't have the time or the energy to research her disease on the Internet, and I could read between the lines of what the doctors were saying, while Emma was taking their advice at face value. It was important to Emma to feel that she could fight her cancer – anything else would have plunged her into despair, and I just couldn't do that to her.

It became clear in January that, despite our best efforts, we were no longer going to be able to manage without some childcare. Emma was too weak to do anything when she was at home, and although I was not going back to work until March, after that I would have to start covering the Grand Prix season again, which meant going away on a regular basis, and we couldn't expect Emma's parents or friends to drop everything every time and help us out. So we decided to hire a nanny initially for three months, to see Emma through to the end of her chemo and the immediate period after when she was trying to recover her strength and I would already have started to travel. Emma organised the whole thing from her hospital bed and quickly narrowed her search down to a young girl called Anona, who was originally from a farming family near Manchester. However, Emma needed to see her and get a feel for the woman who would be looking after her children at such a difficult time, so Anona went in to be interviewed by her in the Whitbread ward at the Middlesex, and, incredibly, because Emma was in a terrible state when she saw her, Anona ended up staying the entire day, which must have been a fairly extraordinary way to be interviewed for a job.

Anona started with us in mid-February and immediately proved herself to be a practical and jolly person whom the kids took to very quickly. Our house wasn't very big, so when I was there, she would live out and come in to lend a hand, but when I was away, she would live in, sleep on a sofabed in the living room and more or less take over the running of the house. The arrangement worked very well, because friends of ours who lived nearby had lent her a small cottage to live in that was in the grounds of their large house.

The children mostly coped incredibly well with not having their mother around, but at times it was undoubtedly difficult and painful for them. There were tears, hugs, a lot of Daddy chats, and a lot of getting the pen and paper out to explain what was happening. Sometimes, Molly, in particular, would say something that was totally incorrect and which was pure speculation on her part, and I would have to explain very firmly why she was wrong to say that. Maisy, on the other hand, was quite quiet during that entire time, and didn't tend to voice her fears in the way that her older, more exuberant sister did. What was vital, throughout, was for me to stay honest and open with them. And to adapt my vocabulary and the way I presented the information to each of the children, so that Sam could comprehend it in his way, Maisy would be able to grasp more intricate information and Molly was able to understand even more complex explanations. The other crucial thing was that when I went upstairs to have a Daddy chat, no child could leave the room until their particular issue or fear was resolved, and no one could enter the room either until that was done. The child had to be able to keep asking 'what does that mean?' until everything was clear. In that way, they would not start to speculate uncontrollably. Because if you don't tell children the truth about something they find frightening, they will automatically conjure up the bleakest scenario, and imagine the worst.

Many of their questions were of a practical nature. Sam, for example, might ask, 'Why can't Mummy come home today?' or 'Why does Mummy come home, then have to go to the hospital straight away?' if Emma had gone neutrapenic and had had to go into Guildford only hours after coming home from the Middlesex. I would have to explain that her blood doesn't always adjust properly after her treatment, so she gets a temperature and has to go into the hospital in Guildford. Or one of the girls would wonder why the treatment made Emma feel worse than before, and I would have to explain again that it makes her weak and tired because it is killing good cells as well as bad cells. I tried very hard always to give them the truth. But what they never asked was, 'What happens if the treatment doesn't work, and the doctors can't make Mummy better?' or, worse, 'Is Mummy going to die?'

I honestly do not know what I would have said if those questions had come up, particularly as their mother was so determined to live. Children take their cues from those they love and trust, and they implicitly trust their parents, at least when they are as young as mine were. They also take their parents for granted, and it absolutely does not occur to them, unless they are explicitly told otherwise, that their mother or father might die, and certainly not soon. So understandably, it never entered my children's heads that their mother might not survive. They were being told that 'The doctors are doing all they can to make Mummy better'; they also saw their mother and their father behaving as if it was all going to be fine; there was no talk of 'We're not sure it's going to work.' So, for them, there was no doubt in their minds that the doctors *were* going to cure their mum. End of story. And the purpose of the Daddy chats was to answer their questions and allay their worries, not go out of my way to tell them things that they hadn't yet asked me about. And because Emma herself seemed convinced that the treatment was going to work, it would have been unthinkable to tell them, in effect, 'Your mum is going to die, but she doesn't know it yet, so, for God's sake, don't say anything.'

Occasionally, particularly when Emma was in the Middlesex, she would be confronted with the reality of what this disease could do to people. She became close to several of the patients there, in particular a young girl whose stomach cancer was so advanced that the tumour removed by the surgeons was the size of a football. Emma was always so positive herself that her optimism and will to live served as a massive tonic for some of the other patients when their spirits fell and fear swept over them. And she was always trying to selflessly support others through their treatment, so much so that, after her death, I got letters from some of the patients telling me how they couldn't believe how extraordinarily caring and reassuring she had been with them and what an incredible person she had been. One morning, though, I went in to collect Emma and found her very upset in a way that I had never seen before. She had befriended a woman whose liver cancer had been in remission for some years but had finally returned, and this woman had died the previous night. Emma had never been so close to someone who had died, and the sight of the nursing staff discreetly pulling the curtains round the bed and the body finally being taken away had understandably shaken her very deeply. How better to hammer home to someone on the cancer ward that death is a very real possibility for every single person in there?

The rawness of January gave way to February and to days which, imperceptibly at first, but then quite noticeably, started to lengthen. I always loathe mid-winter. We live in darkness for most of the day, the world is forever gloomy and so is my mood, and that was never more the case than the winter that Emma was ill. At the start of 2004, I had wondered with some anguish what the year held in store for me, for her, and of course for the children. Would we have another Christmas together? Would 'it' happen this year? Occasionally, I would go up to London for work and turn up looking dishevelled: unshaven, dressed in old jeans and a T-shirt or jumper. Once the children were in bed, I would still spend most evenings with my bottle of wine, my music and my tears, as I had done for weeks on end before Christmas. I was simply drained by what was going on, by the sheer unrelenting routine of it. Then, some time in February, my mood began to lift. This was partly because the end of Emma's treatment was finally in sight – incredibly, she had done almost six months of non-stop chemotherapy – and partly because there is always one day, every year, right at the end of January, when I suddenly notice that the light has changed. From having been flat, it has become more rounded. The landscape has more contours and subtleties of shades. And that immediately makes me feel more optimistic. This year, strangely, was no exception. Although I had this permanent weight on my shoulders, and knew that things weren't going to get any better, I started to feel more able to cope with what lay ahead.

One morning, right at the end of February, I was in the Middlesex with Emma for what was to be her penultimate cycle of chemo. We were waiting for Jeremy Whelan to come and see her on his rounds. He is a tall, rangy man with a permanently jolly manner who talks to his patients as if they are intelligent human beings, rather than sub-normal idiots who only deserve to be patronised, as some doctors still sadly do. As well as being an expert in his field, he is inspiring, kind, and generous with his time, and I shall always be deeply grateful for everything he did for Emma. That morning, he greeted her with his usual jovial 'Hello, how are you today?' and sat down on her bed to hear her answer. She could no longer sit up, so was more or less lying down when she simply replied, 'I can't have any more.' She had said enough, and, hearing this, Dr Whelan clapped his hands together and said, in a very upbeat, straightforward way, 'Yup, I entirely agree. I think that's a very wise decision indeed. You have had more than most people ever take of this treatment. You have done *extremely* well, but it's not going to make any difference to carry on for just that bit more.' He said that, not because he meant to say that she was going to die anyway so what was the point of continuing, but because the chemo had done its job, which was to allow the removal of the primary tumour and it had also stopped the disease in the lungs from growing any further, which would enable surgeons to attempt the removal of the tumours there. So Emma stopped that day. She didn't even stay in for that day's dose. Instead, she was told by Jeremy Whelan to go home, get plenty of rest, get fit, and prepare for the first of the lung operations. Emma packed her bag there and then and I took her home. She slept all the way. She was totally wrung out, both physically and mentally, she was very thin, her skin was completely white and she was incredibly weak. She was now the person who looked the worst on the entire ward, an ironic state of affairs, given her defiance on day one of her treatment when she had announced that she was *never* going to look like that.

Emma's return home coincided with my return to work a week later. I had no choice in the matter because the Grand Prix season was about to get going again with the first two races of the season, first down in Australia, then over in Kuala Lumpur. During the early weeks of 2004, as well as the hammering that her body had taken, Emma's mind had begun to change. And by the time she stopped the chemo and was brought home, I was convinced that the poison that was coursing through her veins affected her mentally and affected her ability to handle any rational thoughts. It was as if her mind had become scrambled, and she would jump frenziedly from one thought to another, in a totally random way, would have wild mood swings and would become terrified because she suddenly doubted her ability to do anything, even simple tasks such as boiling the kettle. Mentally, she was very unstable and that was of serious concern to me and to those around her. And what was more awful was the fact that she too was sometimes aware of her mental fragility and was very scared by it.

During this time, we didn't have any actual arguments, but there was a constant undercurrent of tension between us. And as soon as she got home, having finished her chemo, our relationship started to take a real battering. She would have sleepless nights when she would get up and wander around the house, almost talking to herself in a sort of delirium. One moment, she would get up and make herself a cup of tea, the next she would be blaming me, yet again, for not making it for her. It was incredibly frustrating to be around her because I knew I could never explode and just shout at her for being so difficult. I had to take whatever she threw at me. Yet in all honesty, a part of me actually wished she could go back into hospital so that I could have our well-oiled routine back.

At one stage, I became so confused by what I felt about Emma that I went to see a friend of mine whose own wife had died of breast cancer not long before. I remembered seeing him carry her carefully in his arms and put her to bed during her final weeks when she was in so much pain that she could no longer walk, and I had assumed that he had done this out of boundless love for her because, at that stage, I had also witnessed her being absolutely vile to him, screaming at him and reproaching him for all sorts of little things that he never seemed to do right. Yet he seemed to accept whatever abuse she threw in his direction. I needed to ask him whether, during the darkest times of her illness, his love had ever got shaken in the way that mine now was for Emma. As Graham and I walked around his garden, and he began to reminisce about that awful time, I stopped and turned to him. 'Tell me, Graham, how did you . . .' and before I had finished my question, he said, '. . . love my wife when she had cancer?'

'How did you know I was going to say that?'

'Because it's written all over your face that that's what you wanted to ask.'

'So tell me then.'

'Jon, let me put it like this: if I had to go through that now, the same shit that I went through then, I would have got up and left.'

What he meant was that, if he'd known in advance what he'd have to go through, he wouldn't have put up with it. In fact, I know he would have, because they had two boys, and he would never have hurt them by leaving their mother, but it answered my question. And made me enormously relieved that the feelings I was experiencing were acceptable to have. Other people felt them too, and I wasn't after all the monster I was beginning to think I was. The fact was, the cancer *had* changed Emma, and had changed the way in which I saw her. It wasn't that I didn't love her – I never stopped doing that – but I hated everything to do with the illness and what it had done to her, and to us. And I hated knowing that there was no way out of the situation: I felt as if I was inside a ball that was bouncing down a hill, like a gyroscope, but at the same time I was watching it go down the hill, powerless to stop its progress. It's possible that Emma, too, was saddened by what had become of our relationship, but she was so wrapped up in trying to stay alive that she probably didn't have much time or energy to dwell on the matter.

We had discussed the fact that I would be going away and Emma was in complete agreement. After all, Olympus had been very good to me, and had not minded that I hadn't done any work for them for nearly five months, so I felt I owed it to them to give them something back, in return for their understanding and support. One of the other reasons I felt happy about going away was that the children had very much wanted me to. During the winter, they had regularly asked me, 'You *will* carry on working, won't you, Daddy?' whenever I explained to them why I was taking such a long break. For them, it was important that I kept working, because that represented normality to them, and if I wasn't working, it meant that things were so bad at home that it was impossible for me to go away. So I felt comforted by their desire to see things return to how they had been 'before'. For this forthcoming trip, Emma had arranged for her parents to come over and help, as well as her friend Jo, who had rung up during the guinea pigs incident and who had been fantastically helpful throughout. And, of course, Anona, our new nanny, would also be there.

There were no tears when I left, although it was a wrench for me to leave the kids because during the previous six months, I had hardly been away from them, and we had formed an intensely close bond. On the way, I had a stop-off in Singapore, so I decided to make a quick call home to check everything was okay. Emma picked up the phone. Gone was the quiet tone in which she had bid me goodbye a few hours earlier. 'You bastard,' she shouted viciously down the phone to me. She sounded hysterical with anger. 'How dare you! What the hell do you think you're doing? Get back on a plane and come back home. Now.' And she actually slammed the phone down on me. I quickly dialled our number again and luckily this time Jo, who was now at home, answered. 'It's okay,' she said. 'Emma's gone to sit with the kids. But whatever you do, don't come home, we've got it all under control. She'll be fine, don't worry.' But I was deeply shaken. On the one hand, she had seemed adamant that she wanted us to get back to some semblance of normality as quickly as possible: on the other she now seemed to be saying, 'At the time I need you the most, you've just pushed off and left me.' Once again, it seemed that nothing I did was right. I was completely confused but had no choice but to continue with my trip: I had a job to do, I had immense loyalty to Olympus, and Emma and I had decided together that I should go away. But by the time I put the phone down a second time, I had absolutely hit rock bottom and was close to tears. The winter had taken such an emotional toll on me that I was completely wrung out.

I flew on to Australia with my mind in a spin. When I got there, I called home again, to be told by Jo that Emma had checked herself into our local Macmillan Cancer Care Unit that was attached to the King Edward VII hospital in Midhurst. It had been her decision and although she only spent five days there, I think she knew she had to go in because physically and mentally she too was absolutely at the end of her tether, and she needed the peace and quiet that the hospice offered. She wanted to sleep, to recover a little mental and physical strength, and to be in an environment where all the staff around her understood exactly what she was going through. In addition, now that she had finished her chemo, Emma was actually, for the first time in about nine months, free of the doctors, nurses and assorted medical staff in charge of saving her life. During that time, I think she had become somewhat institutionalised. Suddenly, she was on her own, and her security blanket of round-the-clock medical attention had now evaporated, and I suspect that made her feel very vulnerable, exposed and afraid, hence her outburst over the phone.

It turned out that there was a biological reason for her mental fragility, which Emma was told about when she arrived at the hospice to receive what is called 'respite care', something all hospices aim to provide wherever possible. They assessed her and found that she was suffering from insomnia, acute anxiety and vulnerability. She was showing signs of panic and told the resident counsellor that she felt her mind was blocked and removed from what was going on around her, as if she was in a film that she wasn't part of. She also told Dr Hargreaves, the palliative care specialist in charge of the hospice, that she had been on an anti-sickness drug, Lorazepam, since the previous October to off-set the nausea and sickness caused by the chemotherapy. What he explained to Emma, but I did not actually discover until I began writing this book and went to see him myself, was that this drug also relieves anxiety and insomnia which are extreme, though less well-known, side-effects of chemo, and what had happened was that Emma had gone into withdrawal when that drug had been stopped and, because she was still experiencing the effects of the chemo, the anxiety and insomnia, along with all the other feelings of panic, disorientation and irrationality had come bursting back to the surface. Dr Hargreaves prescribed Emma another drug to combat her insomnia and she received a lot of psychological help while she was in the hospice; but, even without knowing the chemical cause of her behaviour, it was clear to me that Emma was a changed person when she came out of hospital.

Consequently, for the next two weeks, although I called home every day, I dreaded it every time. I was terrified of what she would say to me. Naturally I was concerned about how she was, but there was nothing I could do from where I was to make the situation any better for her. Also, I needed to concentrate on the work I was supposed to be doing, to be in the right frame of mind to do my job properly, and that was difficult to do if I had to use up my mental energy during my conversations with Emma. I was really phoning because I wanted to speak to the kids, whom I missed terribly, but I couldn't escape speaking to Emma as well. And her tone never varied. 'So, had a nice day, then?' she would ask, in a sarcastic way. Or 'Had a good evening, did you?' What could I say? 'No, I'm staying in a shit hotel, fucking cockroaches all over the place, and I'm hating every minute of it.' Even if I had said that, it would *still* have meant that I was having a better time than she was. And that, fundamentally, was the problem. So I just bit my tongue and thought, 'Sorry, I'm here because someone is paying for me to be here, and that is enabling us to continue to live in the way that we do.' It was another no-win situation, really.

By the time I came home, Emma was visibly getting stronger physically, and one morning, about a month after the end of the chemo, I suddenly noticed that her eyebrows and lashes were growing back and that her scalp was no longer all white, but grey because of the stubble of hair just starting to show. Incredibly, Jeremy Whelan took the decision soon after to send Emma to Professor Goldstraw, one of the leading surgeons at London's Royal Marsden Hospital, the specialist cancer hospital down the Fulham Road, to discuss the lung operations. After scanning her, he called us both into his consulting room. The situation was complicated: there were large numbers of tumours across both lungs – we had known this from the start. But no one had ever wanted to tell us how many, because at that stage it had been irrelevant. Now it wasn't, so Professor

Goldstraw told us: Emma had 36 tumours, to be precise. What was more, in the left lung there were two tumours that were larger than the others and they were enveloping the main vein into the bottom of the lung. If he couldn't get those out, there was no point in removing the others and therefore in continuing with the operations. It was a case of going in, getting them all out, or doing nothing. 'My gut feeling,' he said to Emma, 'is that I have to go in. My common sense tells me not to, that it's too dangerous.'

Emma's response was simply, 'Well, you are my surgeon, it's your job, and I'm asking you to go in and do whatever you can to get those tumours out.'

'Okay,' he conceded. 'But I'd like you to have the weekend to think about it and decide what you want me to do. Call me on Monday, and if you want to go ahead, I can do it on Wednesday. The ball is in your court.'

I knew what Emma's decision would be, and sure enough, as we left, she confirmed, 'Well, that was a waste of time, because I'll be phoning him first thing Monday morning to tell him to operate.' But as we got into the car, she turned to me and said, 'Oh, my God, I'm riddled!' She didn't say it with despair in her voice, as if there was no point in carrying on. She said it because, like me, she had been truly shocked by the amount of tumours we had been told she had, so much so that, as I was about to start the engine, she stopped me. 'Can you just wait a minute, I feel really sick.'

I replied that Jeremy Whelan had been right: the number of tumours didn't actually matter. What was important was that they were there, and that they were now going to get them out, hopefully.

I didn't want to get drawn any further into a discussion on the merits of having the operation or not. Personally, I was fed up with the whole thing: the treatment, the operations, the recovery time. We'd been told those tumours had calcified and weren't going to be doing anything more, so why not leave them alone? Furthermore, I didn't want to see Emma chopped up again, I didn't want her to lose lung capacity which she almost inevitably would, because that would then reduce her quality of life and leave her fighting for breath whenever she walked anywhere. I knew she was going to die, and whilst she was feeling great, and getting stronger by the day, I wanted that to continue. The kids were enjoying having their mother back, she was able to interact with them in a way that she hadn't been for months, and I – selfishly, perhaps – wanted it to last as long as possible. And I thought the surgery would throw all that away.

As far as Emma was concerned, it was fantastic that she could now have these operations, because they had seemed so utterly remote a mere nine months before when she had first got her diagnosis. I refused to get drawn into a conversation that involved looking into a future that I knew was never going to happen. On the way home, though, I do remember thinking to myself, and for a nanosecond only, 'Actually she's got a point. Maybe if she gets all those tumours removed, she might just have beaten the odds and beaten this thing. Maybe she's done such a great job that she will prove Cannon wrong, and he'll think thank God he did decide to treat her, because now she's going to be okay. Then, just maybe, we'll be into check-ups and scans every three months, every six. Maybe, just maybe . . .' Then I would quickly come to my senses. What was I thinking!

The following Wednesday, Emma was admitted to the Royal Brompton Hospital, round the corner from the Marsden, to have the operation on her left lung. After Emma went down to theatre, Jo came down and joined me to while away the five or so hours that the surgery would take. As a result, the ordeal of waiting for the surgeon to finish was far less than when I had endured the seven and a half hours of waiting in Stanmore. Jo and I walked up and down the King's Road, did a lot of window shopping, had lunch, and I ended up splashing out on some gorgeous, but expensive Villebrequin swimming shorts for the children. The quality is fantastic, as are the colourful designs, and I thought they would love them and be really useful for the summer.

The next day, with Emma safely out of the operation and sitting up in bed, I went in to see her. Her scar ran from the middle of her chest on the front, curved down her side and back up to almost halfway between her shoulder blades. She was incredibly sore but the nurses had already got her out of bed and on to the bike in her room in an attempt to get her lungs working properly again. Miraculously for her – and even the surgeon was astonished – not much of her lung had needed to be removed, so she had suffered barely a 10 per cent reduction in her overall lung capacity. At least that meant that, once she recovered from the operation, her quality of life would not be affected, which was very good news.

Despite her discomfort, Emma seemed on good form and very upbeat when I visited her. Thinking that she would be pleased, and that it would make for a lighter moment of conversation, I had specifically brought the kids' shorts back in that morning to show her. She took one look and just sneered back, 'The kids will *never* wear those! You must be joking. Can you imagine Sam wearing that? With the netting for his little cobblers?' It was so incredibly hurtful. Yet again, I still couldn't do anything right. I felt utterly humiliated, as if I still didn't know my own children, and she, despite all her long absences, continued to know them best of all.

9

Phoning the Isle of Wight

EMMA CAME HOME just four days later and immediately set to work following the doctor's orders to get fit by doing lots of walking, especially uphill. As it happened, our road was on a steep slope, so she started walking up and down it almost as soon as she got out of the car.

The minute she arrived, she also swept aside the routine that we had developed over the last few months. It was as if she was saying 'Right, this is how we are going to do things now', essentially, going back to the old way of doing things without realising that the children had actually changed and grown up a bit since she had last looked after them. Sam had almost learned to dress himself, Maisy was more organised than ever, laying out all her school things the night before, and all three had gained a greater degree of independence. But Emma wanted to get straight back to running the house, doing things her way, and reclaiming the role that had been snatched from her so brutally and absolutely the previous summer. Clearly, that had hurt her deeply and all she wanted now was to become a full-time mother again, and to devote her life to her children. Part of me thought that was great for her and for the kids because it would be fantastic for them to have their mum back. She could take them to school, accompany them to the beach, give them big birthday parties, just like she used to, and I could get on with my work and have a break from everything that I had had to deal with through the winter. But a part of me was also feeling increasingly overwrought not only by Emma's constant irrational behaviour which continued even after her stay in the hospice but also by the continual snide and sneering comments that she directed at me. Indeed, desperate as she was to claw back her role, they hadn't stopped from the moment she had returned, as if, by undermining me and what I had done on my own, she was showing that she was the rightful and better carer for our children; that, despite my best efforts, I still hadn't done things as she would have done, and her way remained the best.

I realise I was not the one who had the cancer, who had to live through the appalling treatment and wonder if I would live. But I am a human being, nonetheless, with emotions and fears, and what I had had to endure was also difficult and, at times, almost unbearable; I think it was normal to hope that the person who was closest to me occasionally acknowledged what I had been trying to do throughout what was undoubtedly a horrific time. Other people rarely, if ever, asked how I was. The focus of their concerns was always Emma, and how she was coping. Never how was I, or what a good job I was doing. As it happens, I didn't expect them to worry about me, and I certainly wasn't after their sympathy or, worse, their pity. All I wanted was for my wife, during whatever time she had left, very occasionally to show she cared about me.

For months, life had been like a pressure cooker. Every day, I would get up and wait to see how high the pressure gauge would be and what unexpected surprises lay in wait for us that we would then have to deal with. Luckily, up until now, work and the support of certain friends had helped me enormously to let off some of my pent-up tension. Together, they had stopped me from exploding. But now that Emma was home permanently – at least for the foreseeable future – I realised that the tension I had felt when she was in hospital was not necessarily any less acute. Quite the reverse, because the cracks in our relationship caused by her illness were not getting any smaller, and the shift in power between us was now being called into question yet again with her return home, welcome as it was.

By early summer, incredibly, Emma was almost back to her normal self, at least physically. She had put on weight, her hair was growing back – much darker than before – and, when she wore her big sunglasses, she looked the picture of health and glamour. She was due back to have the second lung operation six weeks after the first and, in the meantime, she got people in to repaint the house, she took Maisy and a group of her friends up to the theatre in Wimbledon for her birthday at the end of June, and arranged for the two of us to go out to dinner at some friends of ours, Sarah and Tim, who lived a few miles away. A dinner party! It was almost like old times!

From the start, I wasn't happy about going. The evening felt contrived, because we had never seen these people without our children and theirs also being there, so I didn't fancy the idea of just the four of us sitting around a table. It was the sort of evening that, even in normal circumstances, I would have hated and would have been wound up about going to. Consequently, I was already on edge at the prospect of the evening ahead. As we were leaving for dinner, Emma caught sight of a set of photographs that was sitting in the hallway, waiting to be hung back up now that it had been repainted. They had been given to me by a photographer friend who had shot the Stones for their *Sticky Fingers* album and these photographs featured portraits and a group shot of the Stones. I treasured them and was looking forward to putting them back up.

Halfway through dinner, with the main course barely served up, I can't remember what we were talking about when Emma suddenly snapped. 'Oh, and I can tell you, you're not having those Stones photographs back on the wall.'

'What do you mean? Of course those photographs are going back on the wall!' I spluttered back, appalled. I honestly couldn't believe she had just said that because she knew how much those photographs meant to me.

'Oh no they're not. Not with that ugly son of a bitch Keith Richards.'

And that was it. That was when we both lost control. We started arguing in front of the other couple, totally oblivious to them. Once, Sarah tried to interject. 'Shut up, Sarah,' I replied. 'What the fuck do you know about this, I'm having an argument with my wife, stay out of it,' before eventually standing up and announcing, 'Right, I've had enough, I'm out of here.'

I slammed the front door behind me, walked out into the night, and headed straight into the woods that lined the road. I was absolutely livid with Emma and for what she had done to me, because it almost felt like a stitch-up, as if she had waited to have the protection of being in public before announcing that she didn't want those photographs back on the wall. The reality was, of course, that the photographs were just the touch paper that had finally lit the flame. I had been unable to keep a lid on all the pressure that had slowly, slowly, built up inside me for so many long months and, eventually, what had to happen happened. I erupted.

Sarah came out looking for me and found me on the road. 'I'll take you home,' she said, still looking shocked at what had happened. Eventually, she coaxed me into her car but immediately started to lay on the sympathy. 'I'm so sad, Jon, I can understand what you're going through.' I was in no mood to take this outpouring, so I immediately regretted my decision to accept the lift. 'Let me out, let me out, now.'

'It's okay, I know how hard it must be for you . . .'

'No, you fucking don't. You've got no idea. I'm sorry to shout, Sarah, I feel really terrible, but please, just let me out of the car. Stop!'

So she let me out, and I continued striding home through the woods. Still fuming. Still thinking, 'You can rot for what you said, for what you're planning to do.' I knew I needed to be on my own at that precise moment. I had had 11 months of holding in all my feelings in front of Emma, the children and almost everyone else, and I had absolutely run out of power to rein them in any longer. The violence with which I gave vent to those pent-up emotions was something that even I could not have anticipated. It just happened that Sarah was caught in the crossfire.

Eventually, I emerged from the woods and on to another bit of road and, at that moment, Emma drove up in our car. She got out. 'How dare you!' she immediately launched at me. 'How dare you do that in front of Sarah and Tim . . .' but, before she'd got much further, I turned round and spat at her, 'Oh fuck off, you ugly bitch!'

As soon as the words left my mouth, I thought, 'God, what

have I just said! Jesus. Here is a woman who has just had chemo, who is feeling pretty shit, and I have just said that to her!' That was it. I had definitely and irremediably crossed the line. And I knew it. I got in the car without another word; Emma did the same but just started to cry. And she cried all the way home. I was so angry at myself for having said that, because I knew that I hadn't meant to say she was ugly. Of course not. But this whole thing was so ugly, and it had made me use those words. We had never previously had that sort of confrontation. Our relationship was not based on rows and arguments. We would talk through any problems that came up. But this illness had altered our minds and made us say certain things which we couldn't now take back and it was that, together with the enormous frustration and tension that had been building up for almost a year, which had made me say those terrible words.

We drove back in silence. When we got home, Emma went straight to bed. The next morning, she didn't waste any time in bringing up what had been said the previous night. 'You don't love me anymore, you want me dead. You'd be better off with me dead, wouldn't you? You bastard!'

'No, that's not actually what I meant. You know it's not, but why don't you think . . .'

'No, you don't love me anymore!'

'No, of course I don't love you . . .' and before I had had a chance to finish the sentence, she began to rant at me and completely lost the ability to listen to anything further I was going to say. 'Why don't you ever listen to what I've got to say to you?' I tried to interject. But it was fruitless. She went off into another room, slamming the door, convinced that I no longer loved her, leaving me to feel intensely guilty and sad, as I do to this day, that I was unable to finish the sentence and explain what I had really meant to say. I had intended to say, 'No, of course I don't love you in the same way that I loved you a year ago, or 10 years ago, or when I first met you. Because that's normal! I love you in a completely different way, in a way that I can't explain. We've been through too much for our love to stay the same, but you're my wife, and I will always love you, of course I will!' That's what I had wanted to say to her but I was never given that chance, even at the very end of her life, and now it's too late. That fact will stay with me for ever and will continue to haunt me.

Strangely, a week later, we made love for the first time since the night before she had started treatment, back in August. And afterwards, she turned to me and said, 'I can't believe you can do that to me after what you said last week.' But while we had been making love, all the horror and awfulness of what had been going on had been stripped away from us. What remained was an even deeper, more intense love than before, one which transcended everything else that was happening around us. And although in one sense that was very reassuring, it was also incredibly sad because once again it had been the cancer that had brought these powerful emotions to the surface and had made us realise how much we still loved each other. And it was the cancer that meant that I only ever made love to Emma once more, a few days later.

That argument was a one-off but it did reveal that, whether we liked it or not, our relationship had inevitably suffered as a result of Emma's illness. I'm sure Emma was saddened by what had been said, and was probably thinking that this wasn't how we used to be. And in some ways, we each started to grieve for the way we used to be, to the extent that if, by some miracle, God had come down one day and said, 'Right, Emma, you've had a bloody tough year, sorry about that, but now it's going to be fine, and you can now enjoy the rest of your life,' I like to think we might have been okay in the long term, that our relationship would have survived, but I can't be absolutely certain. There is no doubt it would have taken us a long time to rebuild it. Similarly, I believe this illness affects all couples in some way or other, and that it tests their relationship to such a degree that, in many cases, it causes fault lines that are never fully repaired. Some of those relationships survive despite the cracks, but others sadly do not.

By midsummer, Emma was looking and feeling so well that she astonished everyone. Friends of ours would come up to me and say, 'Isn't Emma doing well! She's incredible. She's going to get better,' as if that was it, the cancer was behind her (and phew, they could all get on with their lives again). I know they were trying to sound up-beat, and clearly in front of her, it was great that they were supportive and encouraging ('God, you look *fantastic!*'), because Emma never gave up fighting and wanting to live. But frankly, when they spoke to me, I could have done without their falsely optimistic gushing. I would have to keep reminding them, like a broken record, 'Yes, but don't forget, she's still got a lung full of tumours, and even if she has them removed, it's still in her body . . .' And whatever stage Emma was at, whether it was getting through the chemo ('Isn't she coping well!' they'd exclaim, perhaps thinking that would bolster me), having her leg operation, or her first lung one, or even later, when things started to go catastrophically downhill, some people would still persist in trying to come up with a positive comment despite what was clearly a negative situation. I know those summer months offered her a temporary reprieve from her suffering, but I also knew full well at the time that nothing was going to change the eventual outcome. But I discovered that it doesn't matter what you tell some people, and you can tell them something until you are red or even blue in the face, those people fundamentally cannot and do not want to hear the true meaning of your words. Some would even ask, 'How do you cope with your wife having lung cancer?'

'She hasn't got lung cancer,' I would have to re-explain patiently. 'She's got bone cancer, but it's moved on from the bones to her lungs.'

Equally, two lungfuls of *secondary* tumours, by most people's reckoning, does not sound great. Yet I lost count of the number of people who were too terrified at the prospect of Emma dying to acknowledge what her diagnosis meant and to be able to talk to me as if they really understood its full implications. I'm not sure whether that's because they were upset at the thought that their friend was going to die, or whether they couldn't face the prospect of premature death itself because it made them fear their own mortality. Probably, it was a combination of both. But it certainly didn't help me, indeed it aggravated me that with those people I was not able to have anything other than a meaningless, 'fluffy' conversation about Emma's 'amazing' progress through her treatment. And I would end up having to interrupt them, not rudely, but firmly, to give them a reality check. Because life really was too short for that sort of thing.

~

In mid-July, Emma was due back at the Royal Brompton hospital to have her second lung operation. This was the final surgical hurdle for her, and she was really up for it. Other than experiencing some numbness in her left hand that made holding a fork a bit difficult, Emma was feeling really well. We both put the numbness down to the ongoing side-effects of the chemo, because we had been warned about possible nerve damage. I had gone to Italy for a couple of days to do some work for Olympus and was due to fly back the evening before her operation, by which time Emma was already in hospital because they had to do some scans on her in preparation for the next day's surgery. Unfortunately, because of a car parking fiasco at Gatwick, it was already well past 11pm when I got to my hotel in Chelsea Harbour, so I thought it was too late to go via the hospital to visit Emma. I then saw I had a message from her on my mobile. Standing casually in the middle of the little sitting room that was off the bedroom, and looking out on to the uninspiring jumble of warehouses that backed on to the river, I dialled her number, hoping that I hadn't woken her. She answered straight away. 'I've just got in. How did the scan go?' I asked.

'It's gone to my head,' she shot back, deadpan.

'Riiight,' I answered slowly, as I leaned instinctively back on the table that was behind me. 'So what does that mean?' I continued.

'It means they're not going to be operating on me tomorrow.'

'Do you want me to come in now?'

'No, it's okay. Jo's here. I'll be fine. I need to get some sleep.'

'Okay, well I'll be there first thing in the morning.'

And after bidding each other goodnight, we hung up. What else was there to say?

I just walked around the room, thoughts rushing through my mind: today was Emma's birthday, her 36th birthday, it was one year to the day since she had been told she had a tumour. One year to the day when I had been stuck in that bloody German hotel, surrounded by bloody planes, unable to get home, having been told by Emma that she had a tumour in her knee. The whole thing was just so outrageous! On her fucking birthday, not even the day after! I just couldn't believe it. All that fucking shit we had already been through. 'Here we go again,' I thought, fighting off my despair. 'She should never have had that first lung operation. Chemo doesn't work in the brain, and it's done exactly what I had been told it would do by the hospital in Indianapolis.' And that was mindblowing and crushing, even though I had been expecting it. 'This is it. This is the end,' I couldn't help but think, 'and somehow I think she knows it too. I know Emma, and her voice was too flat, too expressionless.'

When I went in to collect her the next morning, Emma was still waiting for the doctors to come round and sign her out. The news had clearly knocked her sideways because she looked very glum and very tired. She soon rallied, though. 'Oh, that's a real pain,' she announced to me, 'because it's going to delay the second lung operation.' Even when we got home, and she had to explain to the children what had happened, she was quite matter-of-fact. 'It's gone to my head, so we'll do that operation first, then the second lung operation.' And because she seemed quite calm about it, they took the information at face value, didn't see or understand the dreadful implications (why should they?) and almost shrugged their shoulders. 'Oh, okay,' they more or less said, before running off to play.

The following evening, I walked into the bathroom and saw Emma calmly sitting on the floor rubbing cream into the scar on her leg. She suddenly looked up at me and, out of the blue, told me, almost with a sigh, 'You know what, I think this thing is finally going to get me.'

I looked at her, and was overcome with the same sadness that I had felt when I had seen her crawling across the floor like a wounded animal the previous Christmas. This was an inhuman, impossible situation for her, and I now had three choices: I could either lie to her and say, 'No, no, you'll be fine,' but I think she would have known I was lying; or I could say, 'Yeah, you're right, you're not going to get out of this, let's start planning for the end,' which I think would have destroyed her and would have been unspeakably cruel; or I could say nothing and avoid reaching out for the tiny chink in Emma's armour and ripping it open. I chose the latter. I turned around and walked out.

Incredibly, despite everything she had been through, this was the only occasion, except maybe when she had sat in the car after being told she had 36 secondary lung tumours, when Emma had displayed the slightest doubt that she might not survive, and when she might have been handing me the tiniest glimmer of opportunity to reveal that, finally, we were both thinking along the same lines. Up until now, we had been travelling along parallel lines. In the bathroom, those lines had fleetingly crossed, and I had had the merest fraction of a second in which to make a momentous decision about how I would react to what she had said, and whether we would henceforth travel along the same line together or not. I do not regret taking the route I did. And Emma never mentioned the subject again because I believe her words revealed a very temporary lapse in her continuing belief that she could still survive.

The following day, we saw Jeremy Whelan back at the Middlesex so that he could tell us what the ramifications were of the discovery of tumours in the brain. He looked unusually strained, even though God knows he must be used to delivering appalling news on a regular basis. 'Emma, this development has got very serious consequences for your treatment,' he began. I assumed he would then tell us that there was nothing more they could do for her. 'You actually have two tumours on the top of your head but because of their position, the surgeon I work with at the National Hospital for Neurology and Neurosurgery has agreed to operate, and she'll be able to do so in the next few days.'

'But after that, you'll operate on my lung,' asked Emma, full of hope once again. 'No. I have to tell you that a second lung operation is now completely out of the question. The surgeon at the Royal Brompton has confirmed to me that there is no point now that there are tumours in the brain. They are no longer willing to operate on you.' Emma was having none of it, absolutely none of it. 'How can you say that?' she pressed him. 'When I get rid of this from my brain, and you see how well I respond to that operation, just as I did to the other operations, he's going to *want* to do the second lung operation.'

It was unbelievable to listen to her. Here she was, literally fighting for her life. There was no question of, 'Oh, okay, I'm just going to go home and die.' This woman was desperate and just wanted to be given one more chance. Dr Whelan remained like a brick wall; he wasn't going to give in. The problem was, he soon realised that Emma wasn't going to give in either. She would have sat there all day, if necessary, trying to get him to change his mind. So, as a way of compromising and of bringing the discussion to a close, he diplomatically suggested, 'Well, let's just see how you are after the brain operation, then we'll reassess.' He knew full well, of course, what the chances were of that lung operation ever happening.

Emma had her brain operation a few days later. She was a little low beforehand, as I think we both knew that things weren't looking good. But outwardly she was still displaying the same 'Fine, let's get this done' attitude that she had done all along. The hospital, on Queen's Square in Bloomsbury, is very clean, the staff are great, and it has an air of calmness about it. The operation lasted around five hours, and, although it was a boiling hot day, I ended up wandering around Covent Garden somewhat aimlessly, buying a pair of shoes for myself on impulse, before eventually heading back to the hospital to be told that everything had gone well and Emma was now in recovery. She made such good progress that she came home within a few days and, despite having a scar that ran almost from ear to ear, she seemed relatively well. At first, she wasn't even in pain, and it was only after about a week that fluid started to really build up inside her skull and give her headaches. Even then, they weren't excruciating migraine-like headaches, and I remember standing on the beach at West Wittering with a friend of mine, watching Emma running around, having fun with the kids, splashing around in the water, and thinking, 'Wow, that's incredible, given what you've just been through.'

We had been told that the blood and fluid resulting from the operation would take a few weeks to settle down and that, other than take painkillers when she wanted to, there was not much she could do to speed up the healing process. In mid-August, about a month after the brain operation, and with Emma still in a stable condition, I went off to Spa for the Belgian Grand Prix. Anona, our nanny, had just left us after six months, and Emma had decided to take the kids to stay with four or five other mothers and their children who were all renting a big house on the Isle of Wight. It would be ideal: the other mums could help look after the children and I didn't have to worry about Emma having to cope on her own, particularly as her headaches had started to get much more intense a few days before. I left for Belgium on the Thursday, and Emma drove down to the house the following day. I spoke to her as soon as she arrived and by then her head had become so painful that she said to me, 'Can you talk to the doctor at the race because I want to know what he thinks.'

This was Professor Syd Watkins who is a leading neuro-surgeon and who, famously, was the doctor in attendance when Ayrton Senna had his fatal crash. I had known him for years and he regularly asked after Emma. When I told him about the headaches, he looked at me and said quite calmly, 'Okay, she's probably going to have a fit. You need to make sure the people around her are aware of what's going to happen.'

I immediately called the house, spoke to one of the mums and explained to her what I had just been told. The headaches continued to get worse during the first half of the weekend, but when I spoke to Emma on Sunday morning, she said, 'My right leg has been shaking all night, it's been shaking uncontrollably. I don't know why that is.' 'Okay,' I said, 'I'll call you right back,' and I literally ran right round the paddock – this was now less than two hours before the start of the race – until I found Professor Watkins. I grabbed him and breathlessly explained to him what had been happening. 'Right, she's going to fit today,' he simply replied. 'She needs to make sure she's got somebody with her at all times.'

I rang Emma straight back and told her. 'This is a possibility, the doctor said you just need to be aware of it.'

'Okay, fine,' she replied. But she was clearly alarmed because she then began to fret. 'Oh my God, I don't believe it, why didn't the hospital say that was a possibility. And I don't want the children to see me!' They had already seen the leg tremors and she was desperate to protect them from further distress.

The race got under way; I was halfway round the circuit, in the midst of a swarm of other photographers, when my mobile rang. It was one of Emma's friends, saying 'Jon, you need to come home now, Emma's just had a massive fit!'

My first reaction was 'Fuck, this is the worst circuit to get out of', because if you don't get out before the race finishes, you're in there until ten o'clock at night queuing to get out the car park. It's a total nightmare. So I literally ran to the Ferrari media bus, dumped all my stuff, told the guys who were in there that Emma had had a fit and that I had to go, and started running through the paddock, through the throng of fans milling around everywhere, and on towards the car park. It was like running through treacle because all these stupid Michael Schumacher fans were coming the other way, singing and chanting because he'd just won the race and, with it, his seventh world title. At one point, one guy, who must have been pissed, jabbed his umbrella at me and caught me right in the stomach, totally winding me and knocking me to the ground in the process. I had so much adrenaline coursing through my veins at that precise moment that if I had hit him, I'm convinced I would have killed him, I was that wound up. Instead I just scrambled to my feet and hurled abuse at him as I ran on.

Eventually, after the car park attendant allowed me to drive the wrong way out of the car park, thus saving me a further 10 minutes on my journey, I hurtled down the motorway towards Calais. I called Emma's mobile and got Molly on the end of the phone. She was hysterical and screaming. 'What's happening to Mum? What's happening?' And I felt totally and utterly helpless. I couldn't answer her. No one could. Everything we had worked for had gone out the window because neither Emma nor I had an answer for our terrified children. In fact, at that stage, I couldn't make out whether Emma was even conscious or not. I just knew she was still waiting for an ambulance to take her to hospital. Then Emma got on the phone. 'Oh my God, what's happening to me, what's happening to me!' she kept repeating. 'Are you coming home?'

'Yes, I'm on my way, don't worry, I'll ring you as soon as I get there.' And mercifully, at that moment, the ambulance pulled up and whisked her off.

Poor Molly: she had obviously witnessed everything and, understandably, was very scared and shocked. Driving and crying is never a good thing, but as I sped down the motorway, unstoppable tears streamed down my face as I pictured my daughter, gripped by the sort of fear I never wanted her to experience and which I know she will never forget.

10

The Eye of the Hurricane

EVERY HOUR UNTIL I reached home that evening, I called one of the mums on her mobile so that she could tell me what was going on. Emma had been admitted to A&E and somebody – I'll never know who, but two of the mums in the group happened to be nurses – had somehow explained to them that she had osteosarcoma, and had just had a brain operation, although that much was pretty obvious considering her skull had clearly been sliced in half not long before. But because it was a Sunday, St Mary's Hospital in Newport where she had been taken couldn't get hold of the specialist who had performed the operation. Eventually, some other doctor was found who told the people in Newport to keep her in overnight to allow her brain activity to return to normal. He also reassured them that there was no danger of her fitting again in the immediate future.

I managed to speak to Emma herself that evening and she was astonishingly calm. 'It's fine, I'm just really tired. There's no point in you coming over here right now; come over in the morning.' Which is what I did. I took an early ferry from Portsmouth and was picked up by one of the mums who took me straight to the house. I was able to reassure the children who were waiting anxiously for my arrival, then went on to the hospital to see Emma. She was fast asleep, no doubt because the fit had taken its toll on her, and in fact during the entire time I spent with her, she did not wake up.

I then returned to the house and told the kids that their mum would soon be out of hospital, which they were relieved to hear. Sure enough, the next day, Tuesday, Emma was discharged and reunited with them. Her intention was to stay on until the end of the holiday that weekend, because the hospital in London had said that would be the best thing for her, provided she stayed rested and calm. I, meanwhile, had returned to Haslemere, assuming that Emma and the kids would indeed stay on. Then, on the Thursday, I got a call from one of the mums in the house. 'Jon, we don't think Emma should be here.'

'Why?' I asked, point blank.

'Well, we feel she needs to be at home, or in hospital. So we'd prefer it if you came and got her, to be perfectly honest, because we don't want her to have another fit, and we don't want our children to see it.'

They were supposed to be her friends, and now it felt to me as if they were washing their hands of her in case anything awkward happened 'on their patch'. I was fuming but I had no option but to set off once again and bring home my wife.

When I got there, Emma was in tears. She felt totally let down by these women whom she considered to be close friends of hers, who had seemed to care, but who hadn't seemed to understand that all Emma wanted – in what was clearly going to be her final few months of life – was to share one last holiday with her children, and to give them a few late summer happy memories. But no. These women had now turned round and said, as far as Emma was concerned, 'We don't want you here.' And if that wasn't what they were thinking, but genuinely thought she was better off at home, that's not how it came across to Emma. So even today, although I never let on to any of these mums what I thought of them, I cannot help but be angry on Emma's behalf at how they made her feel and I'm really sorry if that offends anyone.

We left the house as quickly as possible and caught the ferry back to the mainland, with Emma cursing all the way. In fact, she got so upset that, not far into the crossing, her leg suddenly started to shake, as though she was about to have another fit. I was horrified and sent Molly straight up to see the captain, while I stayed with Emma. Immediately, he sent some medical personnel to try to calm her down because if she really had had a fit, the ferry would have had to turn around. The kids, in the meantime, were taken up to the bridge to see the captain who made a tremendous fuss of them, and plied them with ice creams. Actually, that was fantastic, because in their excitement, they forgot what was going on down below; indeed, I still have a photograph of them, grinning like three cats who got the cream, clutching dripping ice creams, and looking as if they didn't have a care in the world.

The doctors did the trick: Emma didn't have a fit, but, as soon as we got home, she went straight to bed, and for the next few days, she didn't leave it. She was not well at all, but, amidst all this, I had to go off to Italy for a week to do some photos, first for Ferrari at their factory, then at the Italian Grand Prix at Monza, near Milan. Emma's parents came over and I went off, anxious and with a heavy heart, knowing that her condition was steadily deteriorating. I called every day to find out how she was, and on one occasion, her parents told me that she had had a minor fit but that, as an indication of how used he now was to seeing his mother unwell, Sam had apparently sat on the end of Emma's bed while she was starting to shake and had carried on watching TV throughout, while munching away on some crisps, clearly unperturbed.

By the time I returned on the following Monday morning, however, she was throwing up the whole time, and was in a huge amount of pain. This was the sickest she had ever been, and she was completely disoriented by the combination of pain, vomiting and nausea which were still, we were told, the consequences of the brain operation and of what was going on inside her skull. But because a lot of blood and fluid remained, they still couldn't scan Emma to see exactly what was going on. All they could do was to give her painkillers, and steroids to reduce the swelling. Except that neither was working sufficiently fast or effectively. Plus, they were making her very sick. It was a desperate situation.

I looked at her that morning and decided, 'If she's like this tomorrow, I'm calling the GP and she's going into hospital, because this is just not fair on her.' She was in so much distress, so much pain, that frankly the thought came back into my head that it was almost inhuman to keep somebody alive under such circumstances. If this was what Emma's life was going to be, she really was better off dead. It wasn't so much that I wanted her to be dead, but I wanted her suffering to end, and that meant she had to die.

The next morning, it was clear that she had to be admitted to hospital as quickly as possible. In the half hour while we waited for the ambulance to arrive to take her to Guildford's

Royal Surrey hospital, I wrote out a bullet-point list of her full medical history relating to her cancer: she's got osteosarcoma, she's had chemo, she's known to this doctor in Guildford, to this one at the Middlesex, to this one in the neurosurgery hospital, and so on, so that the ambulance crew and the A&E staff immediately understood the situation. For me, watching the paramedics help Emma shuffle falteringly down the stairs to the waiting ambulance was the most indescribably awful moment of her entire illness: I felt so incredibly sad for her because I knew, with total certainty, that she would never now be coming back. This was it. She was leaving her home for the final time. And I suspect she knew that too.

Later that day, I had to put a wash on and clear up the mess that had been left behind because we had left in a hurry that morning. I went to the laundry basket and it was absolutely full of Emma's stuff: recently she had been so sick that she had had to change her clothes and bedding several times a day, and they were all now waiting to be washed. I looked at it and knew she was never going to wear this stuff again, so I just grabbed it by the armful, grabbed anything else of hers that was lying around the house, and stuffed it all into a giant bin bag. Why wait? I was going to have to do this eventually, so why not do it now, when the kids weren't around? It was a way of accepting the inevitable and if I could at least make a start on it now, I felt that psychologically it would make things just a tiny bit easier when the real sorting out had to be done later on. I tied the bag up and left it by the door. Soon after, the children came home from school, and Molly immediately spotted the bag. Seeing an Ugg boot poking out, she peered inside the bag to see what else was in there. When she saw her mother's clothes, she went mad at me. 'I can't believe you're throwing away Mum's clothes! She's not even dead yet!' By some miracle, the Ugg boot did actually have a hole in it, so I was able to convince her that they, and the other clothes, really did have to be thrown out. But I knew it had nonetheless been a shock for Molly to see that bag.

The following day, Wednesday, I went in to see Emma who was on a side room in A&E when suddenly she had the most almighty fit. It wasn't like her previous episodes. This time, her whole body tensed up, making her almost sit up in bed, her hands drew themselves right up to her face like claws, and her brain was taken over by an absolutely enormous seizure. 'Oh my God, you're going to die on me!' I immediately thought with horror because I hadn't yet had time to prepare Emma's family and, most importantly, the children. The young doctor who came round at once quickly took me to one side and said, as if I didn't understand the significance of what had just happened, that she had just gone into a coma and that I needed to get everyone here. What he was really saying was that death could well come soon – by lunchtime, even – so I now had to prepare all her closest family for this eventuality.

I called Emma's parents straight away to let them know. 'She's just had a fit, I think you need to come to the hospital,' I simply said. They immediately went in to see her, and that was when I had to explain to them what the situation was. That was undeniably a difficult moment for me and for them, and even though I don't think they were surprised to hear the news, they were nonetheless distraught. I had to leave them at the hospital while I attended to an even more important matter: telling my children.

I decided to speak to them individually so that they could each have the privacy I thought they should have when they heard what I had to say. I had already discussed the possibility of there being more tumours in the brain, so I said to each of them that this was now the likely reason why the swelling was not going down. I had to put the idea into their minds that their mum had put up a great fight, that this was awful, but just to be warned, they now had to know that she was going to die. I didn't know when, it could be tonight, it could be next week, but that was now going to happen.

They were devastated, utterly devastated, although subconsciously they had already realised that things were far from right. But no child wants to hear confirmation that their mother is going to die, and they all tell me now, even Molly who, being the eldest, was probably most aware of what was happening, that until I told them, they had never, ever, really thought that their mother was going to die. They cried, which sadly is a good sign, and they asked a few questions, though not many. But after I had finished telling each child, they sat downstairs, quietly watching TV off and on, while they slowly began to take in the enormity of what they had just been told.

Over the next couple of days, there was precious little change but, by the weekend, Emma showed slight signs of improvement and on the Monday the doctors were finally able to scan her brain. That was when they confirmed to me what they and I had suspected all along: she had five more tumours, and the situation was now totally hopeless. When I spoke again to the same junior doctor who had seen Emma the day she had

had her fit, we decided it was now a question of finding somewhere nice and calm where she could spend her remaining days, pain free and in peace. 'I'd be happy to start now,' I said to him, 'to let her drift away.' I was trying to explain that I didn't want any more medical intervention, other than palliative care, because I desperately didn't want the whole thing dragging on for weeks. I just didn't see the point in prolonging her suffering because she had had two horrific weeks of it as it was. I just wanted everyone to say their goodbyes now, rather than coming in every day and wondering, 'Is it today, is it tomorrow?'

'Okay, point taken,' he replied, 'but she's not going to drift away just like that. She's 36, she's fit and strong, her organs are not affected, and her heart is still pounding away.'

We were very fortunate: within 24 hours, a bed had been found for Emma back at the Macmillan Unit where she had spent a few days the previous March. Hospices are never very big – this one only had 19 beds – and there is always a severe shortage of space. But, like all hospices, it had a wonderful sense of calm and serenity. They do not feel, look or smell like hospitals: they are bright, pleasant places, they are carpeted throughout, and each person has their own room with a TV and a chest of drawers. And the staff are incredible, every single one of them. They are not trying to save patients' lives; they are trying to make sure the time they have left is as good as possible, to give people the dignity they deserve as their life comes to a close, something which, shockingly, is still denied to so many. There are only 3,000 hospice beds in the UK and only 4 per cent of people die in a hospice, which is a tragedy and a disgrace. Emma was one of the very lucky few to be able to die in such a peaceful, caring environment and that is something for which I shall always be deeply grateful.

I met the palliative care consultant, Dr Hargreaves, on the Monday after Emma's arrival at the hospice. I hadn't been able to meet him when Emma had stayed there in March because I had been away in Australia but he immediately struck me as being a friendly, approachable man, someone who was passionate about his job, and cared deeply about the welfare of his patients. I explained to him too that I didn't want them to prolong her life and he reassured me that they would simply let her go at her own pace. He estimated that she might live on for another week or so. In the end, from the day she had her massive seizure in hospital, Emma lived on for another 22 days. But from that day onwards, she never regained full consciousness or uttered a coherent sentence.

Although Emma was not fully conscious during that time, during the first week in the Macmillan Unit she would regularly give signs that she retained an awareness of what was going on around her, and I'm certain she could hear what was being said until almost the very end. She indicated to Dr Hargreaves during that first week that she wanted to continue with her drug routine, which is what he did because it's important that the patient feels in control of the situation, however hopeless it is. So she continued to receive various cocktails of drugs, including steroids to reduce the swelling in her brain, and either morphine or paracetamol delivered intravenously. In addition, a subcutaneous machine delivered an injection of anti-fitting medication at regular intervals. Sometimes, I would ask her, 'Are you in pain?' because her hands and arms had tensed up again like claws and she would answer, 'Yes I am.' I could then ask the nurses to give her an additional morphine injection.

On a lighter note, I could also ask her, 'Do you want a cup of tea?' and she would say, 'Yes please.' She never opened her eyes, but she could still manage to drink it through a straw. Other days, though, she would suddenly come out with a random sentence, which had no bearing on what I had been talking to her about. One day, for example, and for no reason at all, she announced 'Just give me a minute and we'll go shopping!' When I told the children later that evening, in an attempt to grab whatever sliver of humour we could from the situation, 'Hey, you'll never guess what Mum said today? She said she was going to get up and go shopping!' that was so unbelievable to them that they almost wet themselves laughing at the thought. Another time I told them, 'Oh, today I tried to give her a cup of tea, and she just dribbled it down her front. I mean, how rude is that!' and they laughed like hyenas and asked, 'So did you mop it up?' 'Of course I mopped it up!' and they howled away even more. We weren't being insensitive, we were simply trying to find some small element of relief from the undeniable awfulness of the situation. And I'm quite sure that, had she ever, thanks to some ridiculous miracle, woken up and recovered from her illness, Emma would have been the first to laugh with us at what I had said.

I would go in every day to see her after the morning school run, but for the children it was different. They had been to visit her in the Royal Surrey, and that had been very upsetting for them, and for Maisy in particular. She had taken one look at her mother lying in bed surrounded by all sorts of machines and tubes and had walked straight out again, saying, 'I don't like this, I want to go!' In the end, Emma's dad had had to go and find her to comfort her, whilst I had stayed with the other two children. So I definitely wanted to leave it up to them to decide, and certainly didn't want to force them to see their mother days away from death, in the same way as I had been forced to stand at the foot of my father's bed and watch him take virtually his last breath. In the end, Molly and Sam did each go in a couple of times to visit Emma when she was in the hospice, but Maisy never again saw her mother.

One day, just over a week before their mother died, Molly and Sam went in to see her. I had warned them that it would be like in Guildford, that she would not be able to say anything because she was very deeply asleep. But they wanted to see the cards that they and Maisy had carefully drawn for her, and that I had told them Emma had had placed straight in front of her bed so that she could see them all the time. It was important, I felt, that they had the impression they were still a part of their mother's life. As I opened the door, Sam went running straight into the room and said ebulliently, as he saw his mother lying there, motionless and with her eyes closed, 'I love you, Mummy!' And before he had even reached her bed, she replied, quite clearly, 'I love you too.' He then gave her the biggest hug, as did Molly, and although there was no response from Emma, it proved to them that their mother could still hear them. Those were the last words I ever heard Emma speak and the last time Molly and Sam saw their mother. And I look back now and think, 'How lucky is that little boy because that memory will stay with him for ever: the last words his mother ever spoke were to him.'

Like me, Emma's parents went in every day to see their daughter. Her brothers and various other members of her extended family also paid visits, but I always asked that they call me before they did so, because I didn't want a long queue of people there when I was seeing her, and I always insisted that I see her alone. Even her parents had to sit outside while I was in with Emma. However, the fact that they were invariably there when I arrived almost became an issue for me: I felt I couldn't just drop in because they'd be there as well. That said, at the weekends, when I was at home much more with the children, trying to keep life as normal as possible for them, it was great that they could spend several hours a day with her.

My mother and sisters, on the other hand, who had been of no support whatsoever during Emma's illness, did not come down – not that I would have wanted them to. I think my mother visited Emma a couple of times in total during her illness, and my sisters called me once or twice but never came over. Of course, I didn't expect anything from them, and never had done, so why start now? It would have been entirely artificial and hypocritical.

On the other hand, Emma had three friends, Jo, Becca and Gina, her three closest girlfriends whom she had grown up with, and throughout her illness, they had done everything they could to help Emma, either by always being available on the end of a phone, or by visiting and supporting her whenever she was in hospital, or by helping us in practical ways. Now that the end was clearly in sight, Becca, who lived in New York, came over for a week to say her farewells, while Gina and Jo continued to visit on an almost daily basis until a few days before Emma's death. I know Emma spoke to them a lot during the many weeks and months that she was ill, and she found their words very comforting. Emma was incredibly lucky to have them because they proved to be true friends that she could count on, and for that I shall always be truly thankful.

By the final weekend, about 10 days after she had been admitted to the Macmillan Unit, it was fairly obvious that Emma was going downhill fast. The hurricane that I had first seen approaching 14 months before was about to pass over our heads, and Emma's death – the eye of the hurricane – was only days away. 'Let's have a look at how she is on Monday, and we'll make a decision then,' said Dr Hargreaves ominously on the Friday afternoon. Knowing what that meant, I called Emma's closest friends and let them know that now was the time to say their last goodbyes, because after that, I and her parents would like to be left alone with her. For several days now, even though I continued to talk to her, there had been no response from her to anything, no squeezing back when I squeezed her hand, no murmur, no movement. She was very still, very quiet. I knew there was not much time left, so I sat by her bed, holding her hand, and made sure I told her that she had put up a monumental battle and that she should relax now and be peaceful. We were all okay. The kids loved her, I would be fine with them and she shouldn't worry about us. Most of all, I told her that I loved her. I know she heard me.

~

Monday morning came, I had been in to see Emma and was just standing in the corridor outside her room when Dr Hargreaves came up. 'Morning,' he began, deadpan. 'Do you want to come into the office?'

I followed him, my heart immediately pounding away in my chest.

'So, how was the weekend?' he asked me and the nurse on duty.

'Well, there was absolutely nothing. There's been nothing for the last few days, as you know,' I confirmed.

And the nurse added, 'Yes, and the team that was on at the weekend didn't see anything at all, either.'

'Okay, let's go and have a look,' he said. And I followed him back to Emma's room, not knowing what he was going to say or do.

While I stood at the end of the bed, he positioned himself next to Emma and carried out various tests to see if there was any reaction from her to verbal or physical stimulus. Nothing. Finally, addressing not me, but her, because she was still the patient, he said, 'Emma, are you aware of what is happening?' There was no response. Absolutely nothing. He paused for a short while, then he told her gently, 'We are going to stop the steroids, Emma, and by doing so, that means you will die.'

A few seconds went by. Then, suddenly, breaking through the silence, we heard the most terrible scream come out of Emma. What is more, she screamed without moving a single muscle or opening her mouth, and I was so taken aback and horrified that I had to walk out of the room at once. The scream was all the more chilling and shocking because it was clear that she could still hear absolutely everything. She was still fighting, still wanting to live – even now. And although she hadn't reacted to anything for days, she was obviously so angry and appalled at what she had heard the doctor say that she had, with one final effort, gathered up all her remaining strength and powers of communication and channelled them into this one scream that was a mix of utter fury and despair.

II

6.26 p.m.

I WAS STANDING in the corridor taking in the horror of what I had just heard when I saw, coming down the corridor towards me looking tense but determined, one of Emma's close friends. 'What are you doing here?' I asked, bewildered.

'I've come to see Emma.'

'Er, I told you at the weekend that it would be family only from this morning, and that you had to say goodbye to her beforehand. They're stopping the steroids as we speak, so I'm sorry, but you can't now go and see her.'

At this, she exploded. 'How dare you talk to me like that! You've got no right to say that to me.'

I insisted, 'Look, please go. Please!' But she wouldn't accept what I was asking and just sat down on a chair in the corridor, in an act of stubborn defiance.

I was furious and went to find the consultant, Dr Hargreaves. 'Peter, someone's just turned up, she's an old friend, she wants to see Emma but I don't want her to go in.' 'I totally agree. This is now your time, and Emma's parents' time. Nobody else's. We're putting the sign up on the door "family only", so that should be it.'

When I came back, she was still sitting there. She stood up

when she saw me arriving. 'Jon, why won't you let me in? Please!'

In desperation, I turned to Dr Hargreaves. 'Peter, please can you go and have a word with her. I can't bear to speak to her, I'm absolutely on the verge of losing control.' I went to the loo to get away from her for a few minutes but when I came back, she was still talking to Dr Hargreaves. I was so wound up, so unable to deal with this behaviour at such a time that I went in to Emma's room where the nurses were busy taking the superfluous drips out of her arms, leaving her with just the morphine one, and making her as comfortable as possible. Eventually, I decided it just wasn't worth the grief, so I went back out to speak to this friend who was clearly not going to leave. 'Jon, I'm really sorry, but . . .'

'Look,' I interrupted her, uninterested in what she had to say, 'in about 10 minutes, I've got to go and collect the kids. If you want to go in there and say your goodbyes, you can. But that's it. You go in there, kiss her goodbye, then you leave. Is that clear?'

I told the sister to make sure that the goodbye was brief, and left the friend to it. What frustrated me was that she had been unable to understand what I had told her over phone about saying goodbye before Monday morning. I had meant it: after then, it was family only. The doctors had decided less than an hour before that they were now going to withdraw treatment. I now had to get my mind round the fact that this was it: Emma was going to die very soon. I absolutely did not want to clutter my mind with trying to empathise with this friend's pain. That was low on my priority list. Nor did I have time to analyse my reaction to her actions and to work out whether I had upset her.

That too seemed unimportant in the circumstances. I didn't know how little time Emma had left and it was entirely possible that it was a question of a few hours, so I really didn't think her parents and I needed the added aggravation of assorted friends, however close they felt they were, taking up our precious final moments with her. Luckily, I didn't fall out with this friend over the episode, and made up shortly after Emma's death, but I hope she can now understand why I behaved as I did.

I was relieved when Dr Hargreaves decided to withdraw treatment. He had done so because when it is no longer possible to communicate in any way with a patient, then his role is not to prolong the moment of death, but rather to let nature take over. The only medication that was continued was an anti-fitting drug and intravenous paracetamol. Even fluids were stopped that day because they were no longer required. Finally, after a month of waiting, during which Emma's quality of life was very poor, I knew the end was near, and that was a good thing for everyone. No one wants to see their loved ones kept alive in such a manner, and to me, it felt normal and right that, from the moment she had her enormous fit in hospital in Guildford, I should want her death to happen as quickly as possible. It needed to happen. Now that treatment was being withdrawn, we could finally get on with it.

I collected the kids from school and, once we were home, I knew I had to tell them what had been decided that morning. We were all sitting together in the living room and I explained that the doctors had made the decision to stop the steroids because she was going downhill, and that meant she would now die. This was definitely it, and although we didn't know exactly when it would be, it would be soon, in the next few days. The news was less shocking to them than when I had told them a month before that their mother would die. This time, they were expecting it, and they were reconciled to the thought. Even though of course they had no idea how they would feel once she actually did die, for the moment at least, they understood and accepted the situation. I also made a point of asking them whether they wanted to come and see her in the hospice, but none of them did. I had done that every couple of days during the last month, saying in a low-key way, 'I went to see Mum today. Does anyone want to come and see her tomorrow?' so that they had plenty of opportunities to see her. But for me, and I don't care what the so-called experts say, it was vital that they never felt coerced into seeing their mother in the final days and moments of her life. Each family should do what they feel is right for *them*, not right according to what a book or counsellor says. And choosing *not* to see their mother at that stage of her life was what worked for my children.

Tuesday morning was a very stormy, windy morning. It was the beginning of October, and autumn was suddenly kicking in with a vengeance, as if it was mirroring the fast-approaching eye of the hurricane. After dropping the kids at school, I suddenly, on the spur of the moment, decided not to go straight to the hospice but to go windsurfing instead. I badly needed to clear my head and, for me, the best way to do that was to do a solid hour of sailing. Being on the water has always had a really purifying effect for me because it is a time when I can press the pause button on extraneous matters in my life and think about something specific in a totally uninterrupted way. If the sea is relatively calm, I can sail on and on, totally lost in thought, for hours on end, and anything that is in my head has the opportunity to come out – although I often find that I have my greatest moments of deep thoughts when I am about to get hit by a wave. Conversely, if the sea is rough, I can only concentrate on controlling the surfboard and that too has a very cleansing effect on my mind. That morning, I headed for West Wittering because it had always been a special place for me and Emma, so I would feel a particular connection to her by going there. I needed that time on the water just to look up at the sky, to be in an environment I loved and to come to terms with the fact that this was the week when 'it' would finally happen. I wanted to have a small window of time when I could reflect that my life with Emma was about to come to an end, and I also wanted to have a final chance to remember, in a nice way, all the many wonderful moments we had shared: our honeymoon, our holidays together and with the children, buying our house in Haslemere, the birth of the three children and what momentous occasions they had each been. I desperately wanted to have those happy thoughts because I didn't know how long it would be before I would be able to look back at those events with anything other than immense sadness. I wanted to escape, very briefly, from the deep psychological shock that I knew I was about to endure, and the only way I could do that, the only way I could find myself that small period of limbo, was to get out on to the water.

The windsurfing had exactly the desired effect, and by lunchtime, I was all packed up and heading back to the hospital where I spent some time with Emma before collecting the kids once more from school. The next day, with Emma's condition showing no sign of change, I returned to West Wittering for another chance to cleanse my mind.

On Thursday, the weather was still stormy and windy, but for some reason, I decided to go to the hospital first, rather than head straight for the sea. It was just past 9am when I walked into her room and immediately I heard the breathing. That's what told me. Up until now, she had been breathing normally. Now, it was stilted and noisy. She was breathing in sharply, holding her breath, then breathing out sharply a few seconds later. I walked straight out of the room and went to find Dr Hargreaves in his office. 'Would you advise me to sort out the childcare for this afternoon?' was how I put it.

'Yes, I would,' was all he needed to reply.

As I left, Emma's parents were arriving. 'I think this is going to be the day,' I said to them, which came as no surprise. After that, I didn't waste any time. I rushed out of the hospital, rushed round the shops looking like a highly tense contestant from Supermarket Sweep, grabbing various bits and pieces that I knew we were going to need over the next few days once we had battened down the hatches, and rushed home. Once there, I went round each of the kids' rooms throwing the essentials into bags before speeding off once more to the school to await going home time. A couple of mums had already told me that, when the time came, they would look after the children, so, as the kids emerged, I went up to them and said in a very matter-of-fact way, 'Molly, you're going with Jane [Jamieson, a school mum we knew we could count on]; Maisy and Sam, you're going with Sue [Gibbons, another good friend]. You can take the children, *can't you*?' I asked those mums, almost rhetorically, with enough raised eyebrows and emphasis on the last two words to make sure they understood exactly what I was really saying.

'What's going on?' asked the children, slightly taken aback.

'Kids, I think it's going to happen today.'

'Oh, right,' they replied.

'Is that okay?' I carried on, before they had a chance to react further or to get into any long drawn-out discussion. 'Yes? Fine. I'll see you later.'

And with that, I turned round and went back to my car. I didn't think that hanging around was going to help them. It was better to take the drama out of the situation, and to keep things as understated as possible.

I went straight from the school in Fernhurst to the Macmillan Unit which was just up the road, and I was literally pulling up in the hospital car park when my mobile went. It was the nurse in charge of Emma. 'I don't know where you are, but you need to be here, now.' I got out the car, ran down the steps at the end of the car park and on to the path that led round the side of the huge red-bricked Victorian hospital to the entrance of the hospice. As soon as I approached, I saw that the nurse who had called me was standing at the door. That could only mean one thing. 'She's fucking died, hasn't she?' I blurted out breathlessly. She nodded.

I couldn't believe it. I just couldn't believe it. After all the crap I had had to deal with, she hadn't been able to wait. We'd gone through this monumental time together, during all these months. We had seen the whole thing through together. I had been there at the diagnosis, and I wanted to be there with her at the end, to accompany her during her last moments of life. I felt slightly cheated to think that I would not now know what the end had been like for her. I almost had to laugh, it was so ridiculous, to have missed the actual moment after all that. Her parents were just coming out of the room as I was arriving, because she'd apparently been dead for a good five minutes. But as soon as I went in, the most extraordinary thing happened: she suddenly started breathing again. And she actually breathed for another two hours. I don't know if that is really unusual, and I can't explain why it happened – maybe she wanted me there, maybe she was still fighting – but all I can say is that I am pleased I was actually there when she finally did go.

The nurses were coming in every now and again to see if I was okay – at one stage they even gave her a morphine injection to relax her and aid her breathing – while Emma's parents waited patiently outside, allowing me my final moments with my wife. The vicar attached to the hospice came in after a while to sit with me. I think he'd spent the day with her parents, and they had wanted him to be present because they were religious and had derived comfort from their faith. And I was pleased for them that it had helped, even though, as a non-believer, religion did nothing for me. 'Do you mind me being here?' he asked.

'No, it's up to you,' I almost shrugged. Frankly, it made no difference to me whether he was there or not, although I suppose it was quite good to have somebody to talk to.

Suddenly, after about two hours, her breathing changed quite dramatically. She started breathing short, sharp, laboured breaths, every now and again. Then there was one final big, noisy breath. I looked at her and gently said, 'You're off now, aren't you?' And a couple of breaths later, that was it. She had breathed her last. 'Goodbye,' I whispered. 'The kids will be fine, don't worry,' then I kissed her.

'I'll leave you alone for a minute,' the priest said as he quietly left the room. 'It's over. It's actually over,' were my first thoughts. There were no tears, but rather a feeling of instant relief, of peace and quiet. The fight was over. At 6.26pm precisely, on 7 October, 2004, the eye of the hurricane had passed over us.

Already, Emma's skin was starting to look blotchy because the blood was pooling, draining into certain parts of her hands. Dr Hargreaves came in to pronounce her dead, after which the nurses arrived to sort Emma out. I looked at them getting to work on her body, and suddenly came to my senses. 'Shit, I'd better get her rings off before they wheel her off – and while I can still get them off!' I managed to remove her wedding ring, but another ring she was wearing on her hand wouldn't come off. I briefly wondered whether I should leave it, but then I decided Molly or Maisy might want it. So I had to get the soap from the basin and start working up a lather on Emma's hand to get this wretched ring off! I started to joke to the nurse while I was doing it, but really it was the sheer relief that made me see the funny side of the situation. Emma's parents then came in and they, too, seemed relieved that it was finally over. None of us cried or wailed or became hysterical because to some extent, we were all in a state of shock. Emma had died, but we hadn't yet been able to absorb the reality of what that meant.

About an hour later, I decided there was nothing more to do at the hospice, so I might as well head home. That was an odd feeling, after all the months of waiting for this very moment. Walking back along the deserted hospital corridors, I kept thinking, 'This is surreal. It's actually happened.' I got outside and the freezing cold wind hit me across the face. The leaves were swirling around the empty car park, it was pitch dark, and, as I filled my lungs with fresh air, I suddenly remembered, 'You've fucking done it! You've bloody gone and died on me.

Just like you said you would that day I forgot the yogurts!' I wasn't angry; I just couldn't believe it. It was almost comical: her prophecy had come true after all.

I got in the car, started up the engine, and as I drove off, I realised that Emma's death was actually early. All those months before, when she had first been diagnosed, I actually thought she had about 18 months left to live. I had also hoped, when she had recovered so well over the summer from her various treatments, that we might have had another Christmas together. But no, she had died about four months 'early', and I remember being surprised by that. I got home, turned the key in the front door and that is when it hit me: 'How weird, I'm now on my own. How weird is that!'

I didn't call a soul, other than the two mums looking after the children. 'Don't say anything,' I told them both, mindful that my children would doubtless be listening out for the phone ringing and would probably overhear any conversation, 'but Emma has just died. I'll be round in the morning. Business as usual, okay?'

'Yes, no problem,' they replied, careful not to say, 'I'm really sorry, Jon,' or any other give-away words. After I had spoken to them, I had a bath and a glass of wine and went to bed early. It was just as well the children weren't in the house that night because I was totally wiped out, totally drained.

Despite everything that had happened that day, I actually managed to have a reasonably good night's sleep. But the nanosecond I awoke the next morning, I remembered exactly what the situation was. There was no split second when I was able to forget. I knew immediately that I had to tell the children. And that remains the most awful, horrible thing I have ever had to do. It was even harder than when I had had to tell them, over a month before, that their mother was going to die. Waking up, feeling so guilty because I knew I was going to ruin their lives; the fear, the shaking, the realisation that their little lives were never going to be how they were supposed to be, and that it was not meant to be like this; without a doubt, the day I had to tell my children that their mother was dead is the day I will hate for the rest of my life.

By the time I got up, I didn't have much time, because it was vital that I got to the children before they left for school. So I quickly grabbed something to eat, and dashed out. When I arrived at Sue's house, though, I got out of the car slowly. Maisy and Sam must have seen me coming because, as I walked towards the front door, they both came out. Maisy cracked at once and, holding me tightly, kept repeating, 'I want my mummy back, I want my mummy back!' while I just stood there clutching on to Sam who was crying. I could not even thank Sue. We got in the car and left at once. I stopped round the corner and gave them both a big hug. There was no need for words. I then drove another 50 yards to Jane's house where Molly was staying. She too saw me pull up and was peering out of a ground-floor window. She came straight out and hugged me tightly, asked me if her mummy had died, and I said, 'Yes.' Her whole body jolted, then, incredibly, she had the presence of mind to turn round, walk back inside and tell her friend Harriet that her mum had died.

On the way home, I told them what had happened. They asked questions, many of them practical in nature: was Granny there, who had fed the cats? I reassured them and, once home, although it was still early morning, they all got back into their PJs. We then sat on the sofa and hugged each other, in total silence, for what felt like hours. The only movement was that of an arm, occasionally wiping away the tears.

12

Changing Lanes

THE DAY THAT Emma had been diagnosed, I realised I was going to have to change lanes the moment she died, and driving back from the Macmillan Unit, I knew that that moment had finally come. I was no longer having to deal with the illness and how it affected me and the children; instead I was going to have to deal with how it would affect us now that Emma had actually died. The illness was no longer there, but its ramifications were ongoing and simply appeared under a different guise, that of having to deal with the grief. And although the day after Emma's death felt peaceful in many ways – the moment when the eye of the hurricane passes over is always the moment of greatest calm – the aftermath of this hurricane was now going to make itself felt in a way that was every bit as powerful and enveloping as when it was approaching.

For the first 24 hours after Emma's death, it was just me and the children, and our abiding emotion was one of relief. It was over. Every now and again, there were more tears, but mainly we wanted to be quiet and not talk. We barely moved from the sofa all day, preferring simply to sit there all cuddled up together, watching the odd film or bit of TV. 'Do you still want to go down to Cardiff tomorrow morning?' I finally asked them that evening. I had long ago arranged for the three of them to spend the weekend with friends of ours who were going to take the girls to see Avril Lavigne at the Millennium Stadium. Although Sam wasn't going to see her as well, the plan had been for him to go down there for the weekend nonetheless. Molly immediately glared at me and, in a tone of dramatic outrage, replied, 'What do you mean? *I'm* going to Avril Lavigne, whether you like it or not!' Just as she had reacted in dramatic fashion to losing her purse the afternoon her mother had told her she had cancer, she was now expressing complete affront at the notion that she might not go to the concert 'just because' her mother had died the day before. That was typical Molly. Was that her way of dealing with shocking news – to transfer its weight on to another incident – or was it simply that the news was so shocking that she couldn't take it all in? In any event, all three children were adamant that they still wanted to go to Cardiff, which I took to be a good sign, and showed that what they craved above all else at that precise moment was normality. Because the children had made the decision themselves that they wanted to go, I didn't think there would be any 'wobbles' on their part during the weekend; but even if there had been, I reassured myself, they were with good friends who obviously knew the situation, knew the children well and would know how to comfort them.

That meant I had the weekend to mourn for Emma on my own, so I decided to go and see some friends up in London. I remember sitting in their house in Wandsworth just talking and talking, before finally heading off to the King's Road to wander round for several hours in a daze, endlessly thinking to myself, 'How weird is this? My wife just died a couple of days ago!' The rest of the weekend passed by in a haze and on Sunday afternoon, the kids returned, tired, but full of stories about the concert and about everything else they had done, and it was really heartening to see them like this. Later that evening, as she clambered into bed, Maisy's face suddenly burst into the biggest grin I had seen on her for many long months. 'Where did that grin come from?' I teased her. 'Oh Dad, I'm just so glad it's all over!'

I gave her a big hug and said, 'Yeah, you're right,' before turning out the light.

I dreaded calling people to tell them Emma had died and, strangely, have little memory of actually doing so – I don't even remember calling my own mother. In the end, I don't think I had to call many people because they started calling me – news gets around quickly – and I would often ask them if they could tell other friends, to save me having to do so. Before long, I was getting phone calls, flowers, cards and letters, some from people I barely knew. I couldn't reply to any of them; in fact, I could hardly bear to read them, even though I know people sent them with the best of motives. Occasionally, even three years on, I still bump into people I haven't seen for a long time and I say, 'You know Emma died, don't you?' and they reply, 'Oh yes, I sent you a card.' And, of course, I don't remember or their card ended up in the bin, unopened.

Inevitably, there was a funeral to organise and to get through, and I let Emma's parents make all the arrangements, partly because it was something I felt incapable of taking on – the children were my priority and sole focus – and partly because their faith meant that they would derive at least some solace from planning the service for their daughter. It was an important ceremony for them, whereas for me, I viewed it simply as something I had to get through, something that couldn't come soon enough to free me from the limbo period I was currently in. The children went back to school as usual on the Monday after returning from Cardiff, because that, along with the concert, represented a vital element of continuity in their lives. They were also very clear, when I asked them, that they did not want to come to the funeral which was to take place later that week, and that was fine by me because I wanted them to make that decision, not me.

On the day itself, Damon and Georgie Hill had arranged to have a few people back after the funeral, so I dropped the kids off with them in the morning so that they could spend the day at their home, surrounded by other children. I then drove over to the church, St Mary's, Easebourne, not far from Haslemere, where the service would take place. It's a traditional, honey-coloured English country church which, for happy occasions such as weddings and christenings, must provide an idyllic backdrop. For me, though, as I walked up the path towards it, I felt as if I was being led to the scaffold. I knocked nervously on the door of the vicarage next to the church, and the vicar, the same lovely, kind man who had sat with me during Emma's final hours of life, answered the door. 'Come in! Would you like a cup of tea?' he asked. Before disappearing off to boil the kettle, he added, 'Perhaps you would like to see where she is?'

'Well, yeah, all right. Better know where everything is!' I tried to joke, as I followed him into the church itself. Emma's coffin was already there, placed austerely on a stand, surrounded by flowers. There was something deeply shocking about seeing it, knowing what was inside. I had a card from the four of us, and the sheer act of walking over to place it on top of the coffin was incredibly difficult for me to do and, as soon as I had done so, I turned round and walked straight out, not in tears, but incapable of uttering a single word to anyone.

Back in the vicarage, I took up a vantage point just inside the front door, just as Molly and Maisy had done when they had waited for me to collect them the day after Emma had died. From my seat, I could look out and see the mourners arriving, knowing that mercifully they couldn't see me. 'I don't think I can do this,' I told the vicar, as the enormity of what was about to happen really began to shake me.

'Sorry, but you have to! There's no way out,' he replied in a cajoling tone that I'm sure he has had to employ on more than one occasion.

Watching everyone filing in, I couldn't bear the idea of being the centre of attention, of feeling their gaze directed at me for the duration of the service. In the end, the vicar had no choice. 'Come on, we've got to go.' And, like a recalcitrant schoolboy, I slowly followed him out. The entrance to the church from the vicarage is to one side of the altar, which meant that I entered in full view of the entire congregation who were already seated. 'Oh my God,' I realised, in horror, 'they're all looking at me!' I just smiled wryly and blew them all a kiss with both hands before sitting down. Up until now, I had managed to keep my composure. Now, with the service under way, it began to crumble. I barely took any part in the proceedings: I didn't read any lessons – one of Emma's brothers did that – but concentrated instead on trying not to completely fall apart. It was of little use: tears streamed continuously down my face while I simply sat there feeling profoundly sad and numb.

I have little memory of what was said or sung but, eventually, the service came to an end, the pallbearers carried Emma out, and I stayed behind, not moving, unable and unwilling to follow the mourners out. A couple of friends, including Damon and my old friend Paul whose parents lived opposite the Chelsea Arts Club, came up to offer a few words of comfort but I was in no fit state to reply. After a while, the vicar came back in so that I could drive him over to the crematorium. I had asked Emma's parents if I could be alone to accompany her there, and they had agreed because they would be saying their goodbye at the funeral service and knew that, in any event, she would soon be laid to rest in a cemetery near their home.

As I clambered into the car, I turned to the vicar and said, in an attempt at light-heartedness, 'Phew, thank God that's over. I can't believe you made me do that!' It was a brief moment of release from the awful tension of the day. We set off for Guildford Crematorium, me at the wheel, the caped crusader in the shape of the vicar beside me, but because I took a slightly different route from the hearse that had already set off, we ended up not only catching it up but actually driving at snail's pace right behind it. I had rather hoped I would be in front of the vehicle and would arrive before it, but instead found myself getting rather impatient at being held up by my wife as she made her stately progress in the hearse. It did cross my mind to overtake, but I thought that might appear a bit rude in the circumstances. Plus, it could even be dangerous, because the country roads leading to Haslemere are full of traffic and, as a result, accidents occur quite frequently. The last thing I wanted was to collide with my own wife's coffin – who knows what could have happened then? So I bided my time, got to the crematorium safely and said goodbye to Emma one final time as the curtain came round the coffin. It was a slightly strange ending but I had wanted to be the last one to see her off.

We then sped back to the church – I did a quick costume change at home on the way, ditching the jacket and swapping trousers for my old jeans – where I dropped off the vicar, before doing the rounds of the vicarage where Emma's parents were holding a small tea there for relatives, and the village pub where other mourners had gathered. Finally, I was free to go to Damon and Georgie's to be reunited with my children. It was mid-afternoon by the time I got there, I was tired and hungry, but fortunately those few friends who were still there left soon after, which meant I could have a bit to eat and really start to relax. 'Thank *God* that's over!' I exclaimed, as I stretched out on the sofa and started chatting about cars and other easy subjects with Damon. By the time I left, it was gone 8pm and time for the kids to start getting ready for bed. They were fine and had had a nice day playing with their friends, and apart from asking me a few questions about the funeral, they were still insistent that they were glad they hadn't gone. I know everyone says it is a rite of passage that all should attend, but once again, I don't agree with the general consensus. People should do whatever feels right for *their* family, not what people expect them to do. And if the children don't want to go to their parent's funeral, what good will it do to force them?

One of the hardest tasks to undertake after the death of a loved one is going through their belongings and deciding what to keep and what to throw away. There are memories attached to each item; some of the pieces are insignificant in themselves, yet provoke powerful emotions. I used to love Emma wearing a simple pair of jeans and a long, flowing top. I took some pictures of her in Cornwall before we had children when she was wearing just jeans and a plain white T-shirt and her beauty blew me away. Having to sift through every single item of her wardrobe and unearth all these clothes again was not therefore something I was looking forward to doing, yet I knew that if I didn't do the sorting as soon as possible after her death, I would find it almost unbearable to do it later.

One afternoon, about a week after the funeral, I casually announced to the kids, 'By the way, I'm going to have a clear-out of my drawers. You know, while I'm at it, I'm going to be getting rid of some of Mum's clothes. Is there anything you want?' By bringing the subject up like this they weren't shocked at what I was proposing, unlike when Molly had accidentally found the Ugg boots poking out of the bin bag before Emma had died. This time, they soon got into the swing of things, picking out some of her clothes, shrieking, 'God, that top! What was she thinking! That's *got* to go.'

'Sure no one wants it?' I would ask, giving them one last chance. 'Right, okay. Out.'

Other things would get fought over. '*I* want that cashmere top she had.' 'No, *I* want it!' And we would have to negotiate. Sam, for example, ended up with one of her beautiful cashmere cardigans that he likes wearing when he's lolling around on the sofa and which makes him look just like a little old man in a dressing gown.

Before long, the room looked like a bombsite and the children were trying on all the clothes, laughing at how ridiculous they looked, and gradually building up their own little pile of clothes that had belonged to their mother. The only thing I kept for myself was Emma's jewellery, which I will distribute to them when they are a little bit older.

There was one final item which I stumbled across as I was emptying the last of Emma's drawers: a plastic bag containing a jumble of bits and pieces – pens, pencils, a couple of books – which Emma must have taken to the Middlesex when she was going in for her chemo sessions. Hidden amongst them, though, was a notebook, and inside it were the beginnings of a diary that Emma had obviously started to keep. I had known about it at the time but had completely forgotten about its existence. One of her close friends, Gina, had suggested that it might help her: she could write down what was happening to her and what the treatment was, the idea being that it would help her to think about how she felt about things. Not surprisingly, I was unable to stop myself opening the notebook. I had no idea what I would find but what I read made me feel very wretched. She had only written a few pages, covering roughly her first two weeks of treatment. After that, distressingly, her writing soon became illegible, and then the entries stopped altogether, presumably because Emma became increasingly unwell and could barely sit up enough in bed to write. She was probably finding it hard as well to think straight, at least while she was actually in the hospital receiving the chemotherapy. But saddest of all, aside from this physical manifestation of how quickly a young person's body breaks down in the face of the brutality of the treatment, is that, in the diary, Emma wrote about how incredibly guilty she felt; it was all her fault, she felt really guilty that she had ruined everything, but she was grateful for everything I was doing. That last sentiment was particularly painful to read, as well as grimly ironic: why had she written it, yet during the entire time that she was ill, she had been unable to tell me? She had not spoken about these feelings, and nor had I, even though we had both been affected by them. Why? Why did she have to burden herself with so much guilt for so long? She had mentioned it in the early days and I had always told her that it wasn't her fault, that it was ridiculous to feel guilty. But clearly that had made no difference, and reading that made me feel grief-stricken for her, because now it was too late to do anything about it, and to try to reassure and comfort her. I stopped reading the diary before I reached the end, because I knew it would be pointless to continue, as it would only upset me even more. And although I thought about keeping it, I decided to throw it out, along with the hats and scarves that had also been aggressively and angrily thrown out by me that afternoon. All were painful reminders of a time that I never wanted to go back to.

The weeks immediately after Emma's death were a blur. For me, it was a time for turning away from the outside world, a time for staying in the house, and trying to be calm. The only thing I remember was having to keep the routine going for the kids because that was clearly what they craved the most. Their needs were the only thing that mattered, so that meant doing the shopping, the packed lunches, the school run, seeing friends whenever the children wanted to, and generally just getting through the days. We were all in shock and, as a result, we were not yet able to talk about what had happened other than in passing. It would take us a bit longer before we could once more talk about Emma, or for the children to ask me questions about her, so although the Daddy chats continued, they were not as frequent or intense as they had been before Emma's death.

Despite everything they had been subjected to, the children seemed by and large to be coping well with the situation. In contrast, I was sometimes so overwhelmed by emotions that on a couple of occasions I found myself sitting at the kitchen table in floods of tears, with Molly coming in and seeing me. 'Oh Dad, what is it?'

'Oh, I was just thinking about Mum, when she . . .' and I would talk about the particular memory which had come back so violently that it had knocked me sideways. And Molly would put her arms around me as I cried and say gently, 'Yeah, I remember that.' Then she would pull up a chair and we would talk and talk until we both felt better. All three children saw me cry and I never tried to hide my tears from them, because they needed to see me upset, they needed to see me grieving. They then knew it was okay for them to cry as well and to be sad when they talked about their mother. Children take their cue from those around them, and if there is little or no mention of the parent who has died, and no outward sign of grief, it's difficult for them to feel they are allowed to show their emotions.

At the beginning of November, Anona, the nanny we had had earlier in the year, came back for a couple of weeks. She was very upset at what had happened and wanted to spend some time with the children and to help me with interviewing for a new nanny who would start in the New Year: the Grand Prix season was starting in March and I would once again be off travelling the circuit, so I needed someone to stay at home whenever I was away. While Anona was with us, it became clear to me that I needed a short break away to try and clear my head just a little, so I went to Marrakech for four days. Frankly, I could have gone to a desert island for all the difference it made:

I was like a total zombie. For four days, I sat in the small roof garden of the hotel and, other than once going to the market to buy a couple of carpets, I didn't move. Not once. I ate, I slept, and I sat in the sun staring blankly ahead of me. That's how wrecked I was mentally and physically.

I got home and was thrown straight back into the routine: schools, housework, shopping, phone calls, schools, homework, dinner, bath, bed. The phone calls had stopped, as had the offers of help, almost as soon as the funeral was over, despite me specifically asking the vicar to say during the service, 'Thanks for your help and please don't stop!' But now that Emma had been buried, the sad reality was that everyone just got back to their normal lives, partly because they saw me and the kids looking fine, so they told themselves there was no need to ask how we were getting on, and partly because as far as they were concerned, their natural inquisitiveness about Emma's condition had been ended because she was dead, so the film was in effect over. I know that unless people have been in my situation, it's difficult for them to realise how important it is to keep supporting someone after the death of their loved one. But there were times when I felt totally out in the cold because I didn't want to call friends – even my closest ones – because I didn't want to impose on them the burden of my pain. In the end, I subconsciously distanced myself from a lot of people because I isolated myself and didn't ask for their help. As a result, I was left on my own, there was barely any time to think or to get upset about the situation, and all I could do was tough it out, because I was determined to get myself and the children through the immediate period after Emma's death.

I had been so busy rushing around that I suddenly realised, one morning, that Christmas was looming. I was horrified at the thought, and there was absolutely no way I wanted us to spend it at home, with all the memories of the previous year's Christmas – the last with Emma – flooding back during every single excruciating minute of the day. I knew instinctively we had to get away, and to go somewhere that was as far away as possible from the life we were currently leading. In this way, I would have the time to really observe my children and to decide what I felt they each needed emotionally. That was not an easy task but I knew that it would be impossible to achieve it at home in Haslemere, with the daily grind of life, schools, homework, TV and other distractions going on relentlessly.

I decided we would go to Hawaii for four weeks, a place that I had always loved and had continued to visit regularly over the years. I used to joke to the kids that I knew more people on Maui than I did in any other part of the world. What they didn't realise until they got there was that it was true. The kids were really excited to be going, and it gave them something to look forward to, not least because they would be missing the last few days of term. We flew into LA and, as we were landing, the children spotted the famous 'Hollywood' sign perched on the hills nearby, which immediately gave them a real buzz and put them in a great mood as we disembarked. Then, without warning, as we were going through immigration, the woman on the desk who was eyeing up all our passports looked at the children and asked them, matter-of-factly, 'Where's your mother?' Fucking hell, I really hadn't seen that one coming! Of course, she was just checking that I wasn't a man who had kidnapped his children and was spiriting them away to another country, so it was a fair question. But the only reply I could give was, 'She's just died.'

Without a word, she stamped the passports and moved us on. Maisy immediately turned to me. 'Why did she ask that question, Dad? Doesn't she know?'

'Of course she doesn't,' I replied calmly, but I realised in that instant that for the first time since Emma's death we had moved outside the immediate circle of people who knew exactly what our situation was, and from now on, and for many years to come, both I and the children would be confronted with that and other similar questions wherever we went.

The immigration incident was forgotten as soon as we checked into our hotel, with its shimmering pool and enormous rooms. It was right on Santa Monica Beach and was a perfect overnight stop. The next morning, we flew on to Hawaii where I had rented a house owned by a friend of mine. We had actually stayed nearby a few years before when the kids were tiny, and as we drove past, I pointed to a lovely beachside house. 'Look, that's where we stayed last time with Mum. Do you remember?' Probably not, but I wanted to be open and not to avoid mentioning their mother, and the best way of doing that, I thought, was for her name to crop up naturally in the course of conversation.

The house we were in was at the other end of the beach, and, within 15 minutes of arriving, the kids had got into their shorts and were scampering along the sand and into the sea. It was a fantastic sight. Here were these children, all winter white, emotionally and physically exhausted, suddenly plunging into this absolutely gorgeous sea, all 80 degrees of turquoise Pacific Ocean. The palm trees were swaying in the breeze, the sky was postcard blue, everything was divinely perfect, and this swim was cleansing my children of all the horrors of the previous 18 months in a way that nothing or no one back in England could have done.

After the swim, we jumped in the car to go and buy some food. Once again, the contrast with England couldn't have been more marked. Goodbye soulless Tesco's, hello local market selling mouth-watering fresh food. As we were walking down the road, a guy called out from the other side, 'Hey, Jon! Nice to see you back. How are things?' 'Great! Pop over and have a beer!'

Sam looked at me and beamed, 'Dad, you really *do* know everyone!' And from that moment on, we kept bumping into people I knew. Many of them had found out about Emma on the Maui grapevine and, when they saw me, they would simply say, 'God, Jon, I'm really sorry,' or would put an arm round my shoulders and ask, 'Jon, how are you doing?' And at the time, that was exactly what I wanted: acknowledgement of what had happened, but no heavy conversations, no 'What happened? Talk me through it.' I wanted the children to see me reply to these people's questions truthfully, but without any great drama. There was no embarrassment, no winking at people in a 'Don't say anything in front of the children' way. I was making it clear to others how I wanted to handle the situation because I think that's the way it should be: people should take their lead from the bereaved person because it's usually pretty obvious if they want to talk or not. And in my case, at that stage, I didn't want to, but I wasn't shying away from mentioning Emma's death either. I just wanted to be somewhere where I didn't have to spend my entire days talking about it. That was my priority, to be left alone with my kids and to try and enjoy life once more. I wanted to see them moving, laughing, eating good fresh food, having fun in the sun and in the sea. In short, I wanted them to be happy.

Once I saw they were having a great time, I was able to relax as well and before long I had befriended a Canadian couple in the house next door and I was getting more than merry with them most evenings, helped by the particularly lethal version of a Margarita that I concocted. Despite this, I would normally get up with the kids at about 6am because of the jet lag. One morning, however, I was still asleep when Molly came in almost three hours later. I barely managed to open my eyes and caught sight of her peering over me, tut-tutting, 'Oh dear, Daddy got drunk again.' I leaped out of bed – with difficulty, admittedly – thinking, 'Right, that's never going to happen again,' and said to the children, 'Come on, we're off surfing.' And what we did that morning was similar to what we then did for much of the holiday: we would drive over to the other side of the island where we met up with friends, we would all get in the water and we would surf for hours. The kids were all standing up on the boards, laughing, having a fantastic, exhilarating time, and putting all the sadness out of their minds – at least for the time being. It was a truly carefree holiday and it was just what we needed.

When the time came to leave at the beginning of January, I had been watching the children long enough to know that they were strong and that they would be able to cope with whatever lay ahead. I hadn't wanted to talk to them when we were on holiday about what would happen when we got home because we were on the other side of the world, in the middle of the Pacific Ocean, having a blast. However, as we sat in the plane, waiting to take off from Hawaii, I turned to all three of them and said, 'You know, we're going back and we're going to move on. It's not going to be easy, but we're moving on. And there'll be other people who haven't moved on and who are still going to want to go on about it, but we'll try and ignore them. We've had a great time, so let's get on and let's go home really on top of things.'

And they were all unanimous in their reply. 'Yeah, right. Let's go, Dad! Absolutely, definitely!' And that's exactly what we did.

13

A Fresh Start

WE WALKED IN through the front door to find an enormous
heap of letters and cards piled up inside, and were immediately
faced with the prospect of diving straight back into a bottomless
pool of grief and darkness. Before I had had a chance to recover
from being submerged by all the issues we had managed to leave
behind for an entire month, Molly bent down and, without a
word, scooped up every single envelope and solemnly placed
them all in a giant black bin bag. The message was crystal clear.

Stepping back inside the house, I had been thinking, 'I can't go
back in there again, I just can't do it,' because I realised that my
views about continuing to live there had not changed at all since I
had been away: all the good memories I had had of the house had
been obliterated by the bad ones. I couldn't enter the kitchen
without seeing Emma crawling across the floor like a wounded
animal. So I now hated the house and wanted to move instantly.
In fact, I had felt that the moment Emma had died, but because I
didn't think it was fair to uproot the children unless they themselves suggested it, I had said nothing and was waiting for them to
make that decision. It didn't take long. Our new nanny, Jess, had
started with us just after we came back from holiday, and the kids
had instantly bonded with her which was great because they

needed to build a good relationship with the woman who was going to look after them a lot in the next couple of years while I tried to get back to doing some work. Jess was in her mid-20s, fun, lively and easy to get on with. She had been with us less than a week when I asked her one afternoon, 'I wonder if the kids will want to move?' and she replied, 'Well, actually, they've already asked,' which was a measure of how quickly she had gained their trust. Not long after Jess had gone home, and before I'd had a chance to bring the subject up myself, the children sat me down at the kitchen table and said, 'Dad, we've been talking, and we'd like to move.' I didn't need to be asked twice.

I started looking the very next day and only saw three houses before settling on the one we live in today. As soon as I walked in through the gate and saw this cosy cottage that sat in an enormous front and back garden, complete with fabulous, child-friendly lawns, I could see us living there, and I knew this would be perfect as our new home, our new haven. Each of the children would have their own bedroom, I would have a study, the house was in a beautiful village not far from Haslemere with a little village school that Sam and Maisy could walk to, so what more could we want?

The children were very excited about the house but they also had regular moments of doubts about leaving their existing home. 'This is our house,' they would say. 'This is where we lived with Mummy, and we're not going to be here anymore!'

I would have to reassure them, 'Listen, this house isn't going anywhere, it's only five miles away from the new one and we're going to be driving past it every time we go to the dentist across the road, so you'll be able to see it. It's not like we're moving to Cornwall.'

Inevitably, they were pulled in opposite directions: most children are sad to leave the only house they have ever known, however keen they are on the new one; with mine, though, the issues were more complex, and whilst they knew they wanted to move, they were afraid that, by leaving the house, it meant they were in some way leaving their mother behind.

We became the owners of the cottage in April but didn't move in until the end of May, which allowed us to move in gradually. The first thing I did was to put up in the front garden the giant trampoline which had been in our previous garden so that when we took stuff over, the kids could have a bounce around and they could feel that they belonged in their new surroundings. When we did eventually move, the children never once went back to the old house, even though it didn't actually get sold until October, and they never once pined for it. In fact, they now say, 'God, I can't believe we ever lived in that house, it's so little!' In fact, it wasn't exactly little, but even if Emma had been alive, we would have had to move eventually because we had outgrown it.

When we returned from Hawaii, I had to get on with one of the other painful tasks which befalls everyone who has lost their wife or husband: I had to deal with the unending bureaucracy. (And I am still dealing with it now, three years later, trying and failing to obtain the bereavement allowance to which I was entitled but only if I applied for it within 90 days of Emma's death because – silly me – that sort of thing should obviously have been top of my agenda at the time.) So, for example, I had to cancel her mobile phone contract, which led to an insane conversation with a so-called customer service assistant. 'Oh, you can't cancel it for a year,' said the jobsworth young man.

'Well, my wife has just died, so she's not going to be using the phone,' I replied curtly.

'Oh, well, all right, in that case, we will allow you to cancel it early, but there will still be a £35 charge.'

'Why?' I would have asked, if I could have been bothered.

After the mobile was cancelled, I had to go to the bank. The lady behind the desk knew Emma well, because it was a small branch, so as soon as I walked in, she looked at me, I looked at her, and we both knew what I had come in to do. And although I had been fine when I walked in, I suddenly got very upset when I realised that what I was doing, in effect, was deleting somebody with a single signature. It was a shocking moment for me, and I could barely acknowledge the lady as she asked me to sign the relevant forms. It was a brutal reminder that Emma was gradually, irrevocably, being wiped from the face of the earth; I was ending her association with the living world, other than with close friends and family who would continue to remember her, and, just as I had got rid of her clothes, I was now getting rid of the physical manifestations of her existence. Every time I sorted out one more piece of paperwork, she took one more step towards extinction.

A few weeks after we returned from holiday, I noticed that the children were starting to talk about Emma again. Not often, but regularly enough, and without getting upset every time. They sometimes asked me questions about her treatment, wanting more information about something that puzzled them, and at other times would simply bring up a memory or an incident that involved her. I too would make sure I mentioned her whenever it seemed relevant to do so ('How lucky are you to be able to walk to school! Your mother would have loved to do that with you!' 'Yeah, yeah,' they'd reply unperturbed), and I wasn't afraid either, if they were misbehaving – because for a short time they were testing me a bit to see how far they could push things – to say, 'Your mother would never let you get away with that, so don't expect me to.' And that would bring them straight back into line every time. I wanted them to know that I was raising them just as Emma would have done and, in that respect, she was still very much a presence in their lives.

The Daddy chats continued, but tended to occur not so much because one of the children asked me something that needed a private conversation but rather because I would notice a change of mood in that child. I remember Maisy suddenly overreacting and becoming angry about something, and I simply observed and took note for a day or two, by the end of which she had become a little tyrant. 'Right, Maisy, upstairs, let's have a Daddy chat,' I finally said. I wasn't cross, but my tone was obviously one of 'Out with it, we obviously need to talk about it'.

We went up to her room, sat on her bed, and at first she denied there was anything wrong. 'I'm fine, really,' she insisted. I don't think she herself had worked out what the problem was. I persisted, telling her that she wasn't behaving as she usually did, that something was obviously up and, in the end, she burst into tears. 'I'm just missing my Mum!' And that was it: she had come out with something she had been bottling up for two days, perhaps not even consciously. What could I say? I gave her a big hug, and let her cry, let her talk, rather than say, 'Oh, don't worry,

Maisy, it will be all right, let me make you a hot chocolate,' in the vain hope that that would make her feel better.

Whenever one of the children got upset in this way, I would always hear them out, rather than try to sweep their emotions away in embarrassment. Just as they had seen me cry, it was important that they could cry freely in front of me, and tell me about their fears, anxieties and sadness. If they suppressed their emotions, they would fester and come out all the more violently at a later stage – maybe years later. And if they were worried about something, it was vital that they shared their thoughts with me, because if children don't know something, they will always jump to the grimmest conclusion or imagine the worst, and this can often end up terrifying them. When the children asked, for example, whether, during chemotherapy, the enormous bruise that Emma had on her arm hurt, I explained that she had bled because the vein that the Picc line was in had not been strong enough, and the bruise was caused by blood which eventually got absorbed, so it probably didn't hurt. It's just that it would have taken a bit longer to heal because Mummy was unwell. 'And do you remember when the Picc line was in her chest and the bloody cat got hold of it and started to get her claws tangled up in it!'

'Oh, yeah, that was so funny,' they ended up cackling. By presenting the facts with honesty and even finding a vaguely light-hearted side to them – not that that was always possible – the kids no longer dwelt on the issue and did not end up assuming – wrongly – the worst. All this took time and effort and I sometimes had to choke back my own tears as I sat with them explaining whatever needed clarifying, going over past events yet again, thinking all the while, 'God, this is unbelievable.

Here am I, having to do this with these kids.' But I knew I had no choice and that in order for these children to survive emotionally, I had to be absolutely there for them at all times, not only ready to listen to what they had to say, but able to pick up on things that they didn't even know they were going to tell me.

Unfortunately, much as I wanted to spend my entire time with the children, I knew that I was going to have to start working again, and the first Formula 1 race of the season, in Australia, was looming. I had been so distracted by what was going on in our lives that it wasn't until halfway through February that I realised with complete horror that I was going to be away for Sam's sixth birthday, and that there was absolutely nothing I could do about it. I had to go. 'God, Sam, you're not going to believe it,' I confessed, 'the bloody Grand Prix is on the same weekend as your birthday.' And, bless him, he just answered, 'Oh, never mind, Granny will be here.' Which she would be. I duly left – guiltily – at the last possible moment, arriving on the Thursday before the race – and called him on his birthday on the Sunday, which wasn't easy given the time difference because I was calling him late in the evening, after a long day at the circuit, whereas he was just beginning his. He was quiet on the phone, so I tried to cheer him up. 'Are you having your friends over?'

'Yes.'

'Is Granny over as well?'

'Yes.'

'Going to have a big cake?'

'Yes.'

None of his usual, 'Hey, Dad, guess what?' chatty ebullience.

I returned home on Tuesday morning after what felt like an agonisingly long 24-hour flight, and as soon as Sam got in from school that afternoon, he ran straight into my room, didn't even acknowledge me, threw himself straight on to my bed and started sobbing uncontrollably. He was totally and utterly devastated, a little boy who was quite simply distraught that his mum had not been there for his birthday and never would be. It was a really difficult moment for me because there was nothing I could do to bring her back. Our life had to go on without Emma, I had to keep working and that was the reality of what lay ahead. Sam understood that, but it was still a tough truth for a six-year-old to have to grasp.

At the start of the summer term, with our house move imminent, Maisy and Sam started at their new school in the village. I had explained the situation to the teachers in advance but, as before when I had told Molly's school about Emma's illness, I had emphasised that the children did not want to be treated any differently. I took both children in on the first day, and although they were inevitably a bit anxious about their new surroundings, they soon waved me off happily enough. At the end of that day, when I went to collect them, Sam's class teacher took me to one side and revealed to me what had happened that morning: she had been in the process of introducing Sam to his new class when he had stood up, out of the blue, and confidently announced to all around him, 'Hi, my name is Sam and my mother died of cancer.' Not surprisingly, the teacher had been completely awestruck by his words, and by the matter-of-fact way in which he had delivered them.

My trips away stirred up a whole mix of emotions. On the one hand, I was pleased to be going back to work: on the other hand, I missed the children terribly and hated leaving them for any longer than was strictly necessary. But the biggest hurdle to overcome was having to revisit, one by one, all the circuits which I had come to associate with various stages of Emma's illness over the last two seasons. By the time the first race took place in Melbourne in March, many people had heard via the Formula 1 grapevine that Emma had died the previous autumn, so I couldn't avoid talking to them about it. The German Grand Prix in July brought back horrible memories of the time Emma had called to tell me that she had cancer, and I had been stuck in that hellishly hot hotel room overnight, unable to fly back until the next morning. Later in the season, I had to revisit the Hungarian Grand Prix: two years before, this had been the first race I had gone to after we had been given the terrible diagnosis by Stephen Cannon and over the course of that weekend around 200 people had come up to me to offer kind words, sympathy and help, all of which I had found profoundly moving. Finally, the Belgian Grand Prix in Spa in August was the scene of the chilling phone call from the Isle of Wight when I was told that Emma had had an enormous seizure, and I had battled my way through the crowds in an effort to get home as quickly as possible.

All these, and many more scenes, were replayed for me every single time I went to a race, and although it was not easy, it was a necessary way of exorcising the demons that would otherwise have continued to lurk in my mind. For example, walking through the paddock in Spa this time, all I could think about was, 'God, the last time I went through this gate I was actually going the other way, on a mad dash to the car park.' But reliving that memory was a good thing, because it meant I could then put it away in a mental drawer so that the next day when I walked in, I felt I had dealt with the emotion. By confronting those memories head-on, and talking about them to work friends who were with me at the races, I was able, in some small measure, to start to deal with them. If I had been in a work situation that allowed me to push away these issues, they might have been suppressed temporarily but I believe they would probably have surfaced – with a vengeance – much later on. For many people, work proves to be an escape at moments of crisis in their lives. They can bury themselves in it and forget the horror of what else is happening to them. For me, it was neither a release nor a refuge. On the contrary, it obliged me to relive Emma's illness in all its stages. Yet, however painful it was to return to these circuits, I was glad to have been given the opportunity to do so.

Back in England, I was also constantly having to go to places that I associated with Emma, and nowhere was that more the case than when I went back to the Chelsea Arts Club for the first time since she had died. I knew I had to do it sooner or later, and it so happened that, during the summer, I had to meet some friends there. Walking down Old Church Street, my hands felt distinctly clammy and my throat began to tighten in anti-cipation of pushing open the front door of the club. By the time I went inside and sat down in the bar, I was a total wreck. My mind leaped straight back to the countless times when I had been there and Emma, who was still working in the office, would walk past and blow me a kiss or give me a little wave as she rushed around going about her business. The people at the club are like a second family to me, and having to face their questions, their condolences, their compassion, was almost too much for me to bear that day. Yet again, though, I realised I couldn't escape from the ordeal and went through with it in the knowledge that failure to do so would gradually lead me down a path where more and more matters went unresolved.

Despite being aware that I was far from happy and was very clearly still grieving for my wife, I started to go out once again: I went to see friends, went to parties, and generally had a wild time, both on and off the circuit. Sometimes, I would wake up feeling rough the next day and that was due to the alcohol, but other times I would feel really terrible without having had much to drink the night before. One minute I'd be the life and soul of the party, the next I'd be feeling really low, for no obvious reason. Often, several days would go by and I'd be fine, then, suddenly, I would wake up depressed. I didn't have time to analyse it, though, because I was still too busy making sure that the children were all right and coping, that everything ran smoothly at home, and that I was doing the work I was supposed to be doing properly.

At the same time, because I no longer felt married, I was also starting to look at other women and that too made me feel better – albeit fleetingly. 'This is weird,' I would think, 'I can look at that woman across the street and say to my friend, "God, she's gorgeous!" without him going, "How dare you, Jon, you're a married man!"' And that was a really strange feeling. What was even stranger was becoming aware that women were actually looking at me. 'I might be 44, but, yes, she's eyeing me up!' Suddenly to be thrown back into the arena of being available was a really odd feeling. Not that it was unpleasant, and, by the summer, I had had a couple of casual relationships with women. I was absolutely not looking for anything long

term or for a quick mother-substitute for my children – I didn't
need that, and nor did they – and I was also very conscious that
I didn't want to have a whole trail of women coming in one
door and out the other, so invariably I saw them in London,
especially during that first year. Equally, though, I didn't want
to have to hide the issue of other women from the children who
were fully aware that I was going to move on, because I had been
very honest with them. 'Look, I *am* going to have a girlfriend.
But it doesn't mean that I don't love your mum or that I don't
respect her memory. Your mum will always be your mum, I will
always love her; and I will always be your dad, whoever comes
into your life at whatever stage.'

They understood that completely and were always conscious
that I needed to go out, to see people and do things. Indeed, they
would regularly comment encouragingly, 'Dad, we just want
you to be happy,' which they could only say because they felt
secure about what I had told them about their mother and my
feelings towards her.

I had already had to deal with Sam's sixth birthday but, over
the summer of 2005, I would be facing a couple of milestones
that I was not looking forward to. Firstly, our wedding
anniversary on 1 June, followed by Emma's birthday on 19 July.
Those first sets of anniversaries were monumental because I
didn't know what would happen on each of these days which
I saw approaching with some trepidation.

When it came to my wedding anniversary, I had no
intention of mentioning it to the children, and indeed wasn't
even aware that they knew its actual date. Someone may have
told them or they may have come across it at some stage, but in
any event on the morning itself, I was just sitting down to

breakfast when they quietly came up to me and said, 'Dad, here's something for you . . .' before handing over a little present. I was even more astonished when I opened up the parcel to find a T-shirt on which they had written, in big bright letters, 'Keith Richards is great – Neil Young rocks. Happy anniversary!' Immediately tears sprang from my eyes and started streaming down my face. I was totally blown away by my kids and by the courage they had shown: they knew how much this day meant to me and they wanted to show me that they understood. We hugged each other strongly as I wept – the kids were fine, funnily enough – and I realised that the reason I was so upset was not because this day should have been my 15th wedding anniversary; the reason I was crying was that their gesture proved to me that what I was doing with my children was right. The way I was handling them and their emotions was right. That was all that counted – nothing else. And as a result, that incredible, precious moment will be etched in my mind for evermore.

Emma's birthday was something we all knew we were going to have to face, so we decided to mark it properly. I could have made sure that we were all so busy on the day that we hardly had time to think about it but I felt strongly that that would have been wrong: firstly because it wouldn't resolve the issue which we would still have to deal with in future years, and secondly because it would quite simply have been really disrespectful to Emma. On the day itself, all the children had made cards that we put up in the house. We had also decided to buy a tree which we were going to plant in the front garden, by the gate. I had bought a magnolia because it produces beautiful pink and white flowers and, although it grows slowly, I liked the idea of Emma's tree stretching its branches welcomingly over the gate as people arrived. I was just about to go outside to start digging when the children came up with an idea. 'Why don't we write her a card and plant it next to the tree?' So they got to work drawing and writing a lovely card from all of them to their mother. As they opened the front door, they suddenly called out to me, 'Dad, look! There's four flowers! Let's put one of them in with the card for Mum.'

Sure enough, we had this peculiar rose bush just outside the front door which had yet to show any sign of flowering. Yet, that morning, we had woken to find four delicate pink flowers which had blossomed overnight. So the children picked one of the flowers, put it in a little plastic sandwich bag along with the card and placed the little parcel next to the young magnolia tree. I filled the hole back up with earth, watered it, and we all stood there and wished Emma a happy birthday. We had marked the occasion with a little ceremony, which the children loved, and that then liberated us to get on with the rest of the day.

The one other thing I needed to do was to go to Emma's grave. As ever, because I did not intend to force them, I asked the children whether they wanted to accompany me but they all said no, which was fine and I went on my own. I spent a long time standing there, thinking of her, feeling deeply sad for her, for everything that she had had to go through, for the awful, inhuman battle she had fought to survive, and for the fact that she was no longer there to see and enjoy her children to whom she had so wanted to devote her life. Eventually it was time to go, and the last thing I did before leaving Emma was to place on her grave the other three pink roses from our garden. And now, if people ask Sam about the rose bush, he says, 'Oh, you wouldn't believe it, but every single year, on Mum's birthday, four flowers come out. It's amazing!'

And he's right. It never flowers before or after. And we always get four pink roses, never more nor less.

14

Searching for Peace
and Quiet

FROM THE MOMENT Emma was diagnosed, I decided that I would not seek any professional help in the form of counselling for me or the children, nor advice from organisations helping families affected by cancer and bereavement. I knew exactly how I wanted to help my kids deal with the grief of losing their mother and I didn't think that an outside person who didn't know us would be able to offer anything useful. I realise that is just my personal opinion and for many people in my situation, having outside help is a complete godsend, but it seemed to me, during the summer of 2005, that the children were coping well with life without their mother. Of course they were still devastated by her death, and still got upset about it, but most of the time they were able to talk about Emma in a normal, natural way, they seemed to be getting emotionally stronger as the weeks went on, and the Daddy chats had even started to reduce in frequency.

The situation was somewhat different for me, because I still found that every single minute of every single day, when I wasn't thinking about getting the kids to school, or emptying the dishwasher, or rushing to the shops for the second time that day because I'd forgotten something, then bang! It would just hit me. A memory, a conversation, an issue, a scene. Something that reminded me of Emma and of what she had had to go through. Because at that stage, the only way in which I could think of her was ill. I had completely lost the ability to remember her when she was well, and what I had seen her enduring had obliterated every other element of her life. Indeed, for a long time, the only thought that came into my mind, the only memory I had was of Emma taking her last breath. It kept coming back to me, not the immense sadness of that moment, but rather the sheer mechanics of it, of what it had sounded like, where I had been sitting, what had been happening just beforehand. The sheer shock of seeing my wife die meant that the picture of me and Emma in the room just wouldn't go away and would jump back into my mind whenever I wasn't busy doing something else. After a while, this initial flashback gave way to other, equally harsh ones: I would be driving back from Stanmore after the diagnosis, or I would be in my hotel room in Chelsea being told by Emma that the cancer had now spread to her brain; I would also replay in my head certain arguments between us, or certain discussions with doctors. 'Why did he say that?' I would wonder, trying to make sense of a particular conversation. Thoughts would come flying at me like a million random pieces of paper blowing in the wind around my head which I would then catch and try to analyse. I never shied away from these thoughts. On the contrary, I enjoyed having them because I visualised myself with an enormous wall of drawers set against a brilliant blue sky and I had to confront every single issue, thought or memory and deal with them so that I could then put each one away in a drawer.

The problem was that these issues would hurtle towards me when I had no escape, when I was in a restaurant, or driving back from the shops, or sitting out on the circuit not so much waiting for the cars to come speeding round the bend, which I should have been, but remembering instead the time, for example, when Emma was being helped into the ambulance as she left home one final time. But that's what grief does, that's how it works: it keeps coming at you, it constantly catches you unawares, and you have no choice but to deal with it there and then. So I would often have to leave restaurants in a hurry when I was dining with fellow photographers during a race, saying, 'Sorry, I'm going home, I've got to go,' or I would be sitting at traffic lights with tears streaming unstoppably down my face as I tried to address the thought or the issue that had come fluttering out in front of me.

And it didn't matter how often I was confronted by a particular issue, it didn't get any easier to deal with it. Not at that stage, in any event. Nor did I have any control over when I could deal with it either. All I knew was that I had to deal with it straight away. I couldn't just tell myself, 'Oh, just forget about it, think about something else and it will go away,' because it didn't, not then.

During the summer holidays, I managed to keep the children busy by seeing friends, having them over for barbeques, going to the beach and surfing. I hadn't wanted to go away because we were planning to spend Christmas in Hawaii again (we had decided that halfway through our first holiday in Hawaii the previous year), and besides, I wanted to stay at home and have our first proper holiday in our new house. The new school year, however, together with the first signs that the leaves on the trees were changing colour, signalled – as they still do today – the start of the countdown to 7 October, the day of Emma's death. It is a time when nature itself slowly dies and shuts down for the winter, when the increasing autumn gloom echoes the darkness and bleakness of Emma's final few weeks, and this never ceases to affect me. Added to which, that year, I still had two more Grand Prix races to cover, in Japan and China, before I could finally finish once and for all my association with a sport which I had never really enjoyed and with which I had originally become involved simply because I was a good friend of Damon Hill. Unfortunately, these final two races meant that I would be away for the first two weeks of October, and therefore for the first anniversary of Emma's death, and I had to explain that to the children. Fortunately, they accepted the situation because I made it very clear to them that, after this trip, I was finished with Formula 1 and, what was more, I was planning to work as little as possible the following year, 2006, and to be around for them almost all the time. So although they were fine about me going away, I was the one who was dreading the day itself, and not looking forward to being on my own on the other side of the world.

I had to be in Tokyo a few days before the race because I had meetings at the Olympus offices in the capital. Flying out to Japan always knocks me sideways: the jet lag going west to east is always worse than in the other direction, the weather at that time of year is hot and humid, and culturally Japan is *so* totally alien – I hate it when I can't even read a street sign in a country – that it makes me feel completely disorientated. Strangely, I was actually staying at the Park Hyatt hotel, which is featured in the film *Lost in Translation*, and I can vouch for the fact that

I could have played Bill Murray's role to perfection during my time there, which wouldn't have been so bad if I'd come across Scarlett Johansson.

On Wednesday, I travelled with a big group of photographers to Suzuka where the race takes place and which is over 300 miles west of Tokyo. The anniversary of Emma's death was two days later, on the Friday, and I spent much of the time in between thinking, 'What is going to happen, what am I going to be like?' With the time difference, I would be asleep at the actual time she died because it would be nearly 2.30am on Saturday morning, but I was anxious about how I would feel during the lead-up to that time. When I spoke to the children on the phone, they sounded reassuringly settled, chatting happily about what was happening at school, and which friends they were seeing that weekend. I hadn't asked Emma's parents to be with them because I assumed they wanted to spend the day on their own, privately, and I also wanted the kids to continue their normal routine, rather than be confronted by the understandable grief which their grandparents would inevitably be feeling.

Surprisingly, when the day itself finally came, I actually felt all right. For the simple reason that nothing happened. The sun rose, I got up, I was busy setting things up for the race, I was surrounded by people, and the day just slipped by, almost as a non-event. It was a huge relief and it made me realise that, as adults, fear and anticipation of what might happen invariably affect us more than the event itself; and we are also affected more than children by the thought of difficult times ahead.

By the time I flew to Shanghai for the final Grand Prix I was desperate to get home, and my frustration at having to be there was not helped by my computers breaking down, which meant a disastrous end to the season for me. As I flew out of China, which to me feels every bit as incomprehensibly bizarre as Japan, all I could think was, 'Thank God that's over. It's finished, I've done it!'

I was really relieved to get home, knowing that I was now going to be with my children for the foreseeable future. I wanted to give them what they needed, which was for their remaining parent to be there all the time, or nearly. This year had been so full on, as had the previous two, that I now just needed to stop, to take stock and to observe the children. I needed to assess how they were getting on. When I arrived back, Jess, our nanny, said, 'You need to have a word with Maisy, she's being a bit funny at the moment.'

So we had a Daddy chat. 'What's up, Maisy?'

'Nothing.'

'No, what's up?'

Eventually, after a bit more coaxing, she suddenly confessed. 'Dad, I've seen Mum.'

'Really?' I replied, trying not to sound shocked. 'Tell me all about it.'

'Well, a couple of nights ago, I was asleep, and I felt somebody shaking my leg. And there was Mum.'

'And, how was she?' I urged her on.

'Well, it's really weird, because it wasn't all of her. It was only her top half. Her hair had grown back, and she was in this sort of ball, this swirling sort of ball. And she was fine.'

'What did you do?'

'Oh, we came downstairs and we went to this lake. And Mum rowed this boat around the lake. I don't know where it was, but there was this white, bright sky all around. She asked me how we were and everything, so I told her.'

'That's fantastic, brilliant,' I said and, because Maisy seemed much happier now that she had told me, I decided to leave it at that.

The next day, I was doing tea and Maisy came in and said, quite casually, 'Oh, by the way, Dad, I saw Mum again last night. This time, she was knocking on the door, so I just came downstairs and let her in, and we had a little chat. Then I went back to bed.'

So then I said, 'Okay, Maisy, sit down. I too have had this experience.'

And I told her how, shortly before I had finally sold the house in Haslemere, which wasn't until the end of September, just before going to Japan, I had gone round there unexpectedly to pick up some post and a few other bits and pieces. I was on auto-pilot: I had opened the front door, and was about to bound up the stairs on my way to my office in the loft when suddenly this *thing* came flying past me. It was like a big swirling ball. It went halfway down the hall before turning round. And it was Emma. Just her head. I physically saw her. And she shouted down the hall, 'What are you *doing* here? Why can't you leave me alone?' before disappearing up the stairs. So I went rushing up the stairs to find her and to have it out with her. I looked in all the rooms but they were completely empty, so after grabbing what I needed from my office, I headed back downstairs, stood in the hall, and shouted, 'I'm leaving now,' before slamming shut the front door.

The following day, having spoken to Emma's friend Gina about the experience, I decided that she must have been trapped and needed to get out before the new owners moved in, so I went back to the house, walked in, and there was a completely different atmosphere. The day before, it had felt highly charged and disturbed, whereas now, everything felt calm and at peace. I walked around the house and eventually said, 'Look, if you're here, I need to tell you something.' Nothing. 'I just have to let you know that this house is now sold. New people are moving in in three weeks, so you need to move on. Cross the line, go wherever you need to go, but leave. You know where we're living, pack your bags and get down the road, because you can't stay here. I know it's sad because this is your home, but you need to leave.'

When I had finished telling my story to Maisy, she was all agog. 'Wow, Dad, that's amazing!'

Then, I suddenly remembered that Sam had come running down the stairs one morning, not that long before, and said, 'I'm just getting my cereal. I'm going to take it upstairs because I'm talking to Mum.'

'Sam?' I managed to ask, astounded.

'Yes, Mum's upstairs so I'm just getting my cereal. I'll be back,' he announced, before charging back up again.

I decided to get Molly and Sam in so that Maisy and I could tell them what we had seen. I fully expected Molly to react in her typically dramatic fashion, 'Oh my God, ghosts, I don't belieeeeve it, in this house!' but instead she announced, 'Well, actually, I did see this woman in the corner of my room, but I didn't even go there. I just rolled over and went back to sleep.'

So that was it. We were all convinced that we had seen Emma, and to us it felt like the most normal thing in the world. None of the children was frightened by what they had seen.

Indeed, they welcomed the idea that their mum was still around in this way. Obviously, no one can explain what happened, but I do believe to this day, as do the children, that Emma was present for each of us. Interestingly, since then, none of us has heard or seen a thing. And no, I don't know what that means either.

The New Year came – Christmas in Hawaii was once again fantastic – and, having turned the corner of midwinter, by spring, we were well established in our routine. I was acutely aware that, in order to really thrive, the children needed to eat healthily, they needed to be in a calm environment and to feel that their life was, inasmuch as that was possible, regular and normal. I loved being around them, and they loved that I was with them as well. Despite this, my wall full of drawers was still a constant presence, and the issues, thoughts and memories were still bombarding me so relentlessly and so hard that I began to think, 'Fucking hell, I've still got the same thoughts coming through my head, the same questions, when is this ever going to stop? When am I going to be able to control them? What's happening, am I going mad? What do I need to do to make them stop?' I could see why people couldn't cope with bereavement, got very depressed, and in the end were driven mad with grief.

I myself had days when I felt really low. I would be having a great time for a week then, inexplicably, I would wake up one morning with an intense sensation that I can only describe as 'feeling like shit'. There was nothing I could put my finger on, but I would look at myself in the mirror and think, 'God, you're not happy.' I wasn't smiling, I was going through the motions, toughing it out, and sometimes even – if I was feeling particularly terrible – I would have to say to the kids, 'I'm feeling a bit shit,' so that they understood why I was quieter than usual.

~

One day, about 18 months after Emma had died, we were all outside. It was a glorious April day, the sort that makes you feel that summer is already upon you, even though you know full well that it can't last and that, before too long, it will be back to showers, wind and grey skies. But the shrubs and flowers had bloomed, the blossom was out on the trees, and the world seemed like a much warmer, more welcoming place. The kids had some friends round and were running around, full of the joys of spring, shrieking away as children do when they play without a care in the world. And I suddenly looked at them, and said to myself, 'These kids are fine. They're all right, they're going to cope. I've done it. I've done what I set out to do, over two and a half years ago when Emma first got ill. But what about you? How are *you*?'

What a mistake to ask myself that. Because literally within 30 seconds, I felt as if I'd been tied to the railway line and coming round the corner towards me was this enormous express train which, in effect, had been gathering steam for all that time and which was about to absolutely flatten me.

I went straight inside and called my friend Pete, one of my handful of friends whom I had really been able to count on in my darkest moments. 'Pete, you'd better get over here, because I'm just about to feel very seriously shit.'

And he came straight over, bringing a few beers with him for good measure, and we talked and talked while the kids carried on playing, mercifully without noticing a thing. I realised that because I had been using up all my energies on the children and on making sure they were coping, I had neglected to look after myself. I also realised that I had no idea how long my deep, intense sadness would last nor whether it was normal that, if anything, these moods were getting worse and more frequent as time went on. I felt completely bewildered by these thoughts and decided, after speaking to Pete, that, although so far I hadn't felt the urge to speak to a counsellor because I had been able to cope on my own, I was now in real need of someone to talk to, so that they could maybe shed some light on what on earth was happening to me.

The next morning I made an appointment to see Kim, a bereavement counsellor who was a friend of Sarah, the woman whose house I had so unceremoniously stormed out of during my appalling row with Emma, and a few days later, I found myself sitting in her office. I told her about everything that had happened before and since Emma's death; I also told her what I had been doing with the kids, how they were and how I was. I wasn't looking for bereavement counselling as such. I knew that I was an emotionally resilient person – I had become that through everything that had happened to me from my child-hood onwards – but I did have the burning need to find out whether what I was now feeling was normal. Everything I had planned from the day of diagnosis had happened, and I had managed to get the children to a certain stage where they were fine – but was I? After Kim finished listening to me, she looked at me and said, 'You know what? I can't offer you any advice, even if you're asking for some. But what I will tell you is that you need to be aware that your lows are going to get more frequent, and they're going to get deeper, and you'd better have people around you who can cope, because you're going to feel unbelievably low. You can't fight the lows and they're going to get worse before they start to get better.'

She then went on to explain that this 'thing' will be with me for ever, it's never going to go away, but eventually I will learn to live alongside it and be able to control it when it hits me. I will be able to push aside the issues and thoughts and memories which are fluttering around my head and will be able to deal with them when it's convenient to do so, rather than there and then. 'Then, you will wake up one day,' she added, because I had told her that I was not getting a single happy memory coming back to me even after all this time, 'and you will suddenly realise that you have had a good memory, or thought. And that will be the moment you start to heal. It doesn't stop the grieving, but it starts to shift the balance in favour of positive thoughts and healing.'

What she told me came as an enormous relief because I had got the explanation I had been looking for, and the reassurance that what I was feeling was normal. I knew, from that moment on, that I would be able to cope with the lows when they happened, however awful, because they were now an inevitable part of the grieving process, and that one day – Kim couldn't tell me when – I would also be able to think of Emma in some way other than with unmitigated sorrow.

About a month after my talk with Kim, I was speaking to Pete again and telling him how low I was feeling (I had realised that I needed to learn to pick up the phone and actually *tell* my friends how I was feeling, rather than wait for them to ask) and he suddenly said to me, 'Why don't you go away? Take a break, take a holiday. I run these windsurfing courses in Egypt. You don't need to do the course but just come anyway.' And that's exactly what I did. Except that Mike, one of the other great guys I had always been able to count on, came along as well, saying, 'I think you need someone else with you, someone to keep an eye on you when Pete is busy running his course.'

I hardly did any surfing that week – my excuse was that there was hardly a breath of wind – but I did get through a steady flow of beers during the day, sitting on my sun lounger, just thinking and recharging my batteries. Pete and Mike, like guardian angels, were there when I wanted them, but they also had the intelligence to just let me be, to let me sit on the beach on my own, feeling like shit – which I did for much of that week – because they realised I had to go through that process. And it did me a lot of good not to have to get up in the morning and worry about the kids, the house, and everything else that took up so much of my daily thought process. It allowed me to stand back, and to take stock of where I was. As a result, it was while I was away that week that I decided I needed to have a fairly radical clear-out in my life, because it presented enough challenges as it was without it being cluttered up by people I didn't want to see anymore, by work issues that were causing me unnecessary strain, and by smaller, mundane issues which were taking up a lot of my energy.

One of the key decisions involved no longer wanting to cope with certain people's inability to deal with Emma's death. I had had so much rubbish to deal with in the last three years that I badly wanted peace and quiet, because that would provide me with the healing environment I now needed. Unfortunately, there were some people, women in particular, mums we knew from the children's schools, for example, who could still only talk about Emma whenever they called me. Having asked how I and the children were coping, they would then launch into long laments of how much they still missed her, and how devastated they had been by her death. One mum actually said to me, 'Every day I think about all those years when we were bringing up our children together, all those walks in the park, and now she's not here, and . . .' and I had to cut her off and say to her, 'Look, you have to stop ringing me and talking about Emma. You need to go away and deal with it. We'll remain friends because of the children, but the relationship between us is going to have to change.' And she was quite shocked by my frankness, but I really couldn't stand listening to her any more.

I was even more frank with a group of mums who, I believe, had mostly proved themselves to be fairly useless when it came to helping Emma, despite professing to be good friends of hers (a couple had been on the fateful Isle of Wight week when Emma had had her fit). One day, during the summer, they had arranged for my children to go over to one of their houses so that they could spend the day with the other kids. That was all very well, but it was all too little, too late, and when I came to collect mine later that afternoon, I stood in amazement as the mothers began to gush, 'Oh Jon, the kids are *so* wonderful, you've done such a great job!'

'Right,' I thought, 'either I say nothing, and this sits in my mind, cluttering it up with angry thoughts, or I say what I have long meant to say.'

In my typically forthright manner, I chose the latter option. 'Yes, well, no great thanks to you,' I replied, to their incredulity.

When I finished giving these women a long-overdue piece of

my mind, several of them were in tears and unable to speak. I gathered up my kids and left soon after, and although I have seen some of them around Haslemere, it's fair to say that my relationship with them ended that day, which is absolutely fine by me, because by severing my ties with these people, I was simplifying my life and making it calmer, and doing that would contribute in the long term to my happiness and to that of my children.

At home, also, I made a determined effort to avoid getting stressed out about little things, such as who had got whose shoe, whether Maisy had pinched Molly's swimming costume or whether Sam had hit Maisy because she'd just beaten him at snap. I once got so annoyed by those petty arguments that I declared, to the kids' astonishment, 'Right, I can't deal with this, it's all too much for me,' before striding off, and ever since then, when I tell them to deal with their arguments themselves, Molly in particular turns round and says, 'Oh, Dad's going to have an "I can't cope" moment.' But she and the other two know, as do I, that if I get stressed, I get low. So wherever possible, I try to stay calm and to conserve my energy not only for fun things, like taking the kids down to the beach, but also for the important or difficult moments in our life.

I remain constantly on the lookout for times when my children might seem down or worried. If one of them is spending an unusual amount of time upstairs in their room, for example, I might call upstairs, 'Are you all right?'

'Yeah, yeah,' comes the answer.

'Yes, but are you all right?'

'Yeah, it's fine, I don't *need* a Daddy chat,' replies that child, sometimes now with a bored intonation, fully aware that that is, in effect, what I am asking.

When Molly was approaching her 13th birthday, in August 2006, it did occur to me that this might cause a hiccup, even though she is not the sort to dwell on things, tends to get on with life, and was showing no signs of being upset in the lead-up to the day. But, suddenly, the evening before her birthday, she came into my room in tears. The emotion had obviously just surfaced. 'I'm really upset, my mum's not going to be here to see me turning 13,' she sobbed, as I hugged her. And I had to let her offload all the grief she had inside her until she felt better. But one of the points I had to make, however much it pained me to do so, was that she had to be aware that this feeling of missing her mum would not be a one-off. It would hit her at all the major stages in her life, when she turned 18, when she got married or had her first baby; each time, she was going to have to accept that this feeling of immense sadness and loss was inevitable and would be with her for ever. But if she was prepared for it, and was able to talk about it – hence the ongoing importance of our Daddy chats – then it might not bite her quite as hard every time it returned.

At least Molly, and Maisy to a certain extent, was old enough to understand what I was trying to explain to her, and to work out why she was sometimes still getting upset. With her little brother, Sam, who was only seven and a half years old, the issue was more complicated, simply because he was that much younger which made it harder for him to work out what was upsetting him; plus, he had a much smaller bank of memories of his mother – as I was about to discover.

15

The Stormy Night

SAM HAD SETTLED well into our village school and was embarking on his second full year there when he started to behave in an uncharacteristically aggressive way, both at home and at school, as if he was permanently in a bad mood. It wasn't as if I could put it down to him being tired, because the new school year had only just started. His teacher asked me if I could have a chat with him, which I did, but he was very defiant and I got absolutely nothing out of him. I was worried that he was brooding over the fact that the second anniversary of his mother's death was approaching, so I explained this to his teacher. 'I'm trying to keep it low-key this year, to see how the kids handle it without me bringing it up.'

That was fine, she said, but he was still being very difficult, and had even started picking on another kid, which was so completely unacceptable in my eyes that I had to come down hard on him.

'Your mother would have been devastated to know that you were being horrible to this kid, that is absolutely not what we're about in this family, and I want you to stop that at once,' which of course made him burst into floods of tears, but changed nothing in his underlying belligerent mood. 'Leave it to me,' I said to the teacher, 'I'll sort it out.'

I went to see a child psychologist who was based at the Macmillan Unit where Emma had been. As with Kim, the bereavement counsellor I had seen six months earlier, I wasn't looking for long-term advice on how to deal with my kids, but I did feel the need to seek her opinion on whether I was doing the right thing with them and whether she had any clue about what was happening to Sam. She quickly reassured me that what I was doing with them was spot on and that they sounded great. 'And if you want me to come to the house to see how they are, I'm more than willing to do that.' So I suggested that to them and they unanimously replied, 'No! Why would we want to talk to her? She doesn't even know us.' Which is why I don't always feel that counselling is the answer to everyone's problems, because the children involved have to want to see the counsellor and have to feel they are going to get something out of the meetings, otherwise everyone is going to be wasting their time. Before I had left her that day, however, the psychologist had asked me whether Sam liked drawing.

'Yes, he draws all the time.'

'Well, get him to do a drawing.'

That evening, when I was in the kitchen, cooking, and Sam was sitting at the kitchen table, I suggested to him, 'Why don't you do a drawing of the family?' So he immediately settled down to the task. A few minutes later, he got off his chair, started walking across the kitchen brandishing his drawing and proudly held it out for me to look at. But before I'd had a chance to catch anything more than a glimpse of it, he snatched it away again and ran back to the table. 'Sam, what are you doing? I want to see the picture.'

'I've forgotten Mum!' he shot back.

Bang! Of course!

'Okay, pop her in the drawing and bring it over,' I replied calmly. And that's exactly what he did. He drew his family with five people in it.

The incident shocked and upset him, though, and he was soon sobbing that he'd forgotten his mum and that he couldn't really remember her. I hugged him hard but, inside me, I was feeling sick at how awful it must be for this little boy to realise he was struggling to hold on to any memory of his mum. What a terrible thing to happen. But the fact was, he had spent so much less time with her than his sisters. His memory bank was small, Maisy's was a bit larger, Molly's was larger still, whilst mine of course was the largest of all.

I picked up the phone immediately to the psychologist. 'Right, he's done the drawing. I've got to the bottom of it: he's forgotten his mum.'

She then told me that from now on it was vital to bolster his memory as much as possible and rebuild it for him, so that he could then start to fill his bank up once more. 'Thanks, you've been great,' I told her. 'I know exactly what to do now.'

And from that moment on, I got the conversations going, got the anecdotes going, without being too heavy handed and obvious about it, but I made sure that his mum was mentioned in a way that kick-started some memories again and put them back into his mind so that he couldn't forget them again. So I'd say, 'Oh, do you remember when we were climbing up that waterfall and Mum nearly dropped you 20 feet into the pool below?'

'Yeah, I do.'

'And then Mum went into the bushes and had a pee and hoped that nobody was looking?'

'Yeah, that was so funny!'

I also told the girls, 'Listen, Sam has been like this because he can't remember his mum,' and we collectively made the decision to involve him, to talk about a funny time or a particular incident and to encourage him to ask questions about what she was like. I also, as I do to this day, pointed out places which their mum and I used to go to, and I showed them round the Chelsea Arts Club, for example. 'This is where Mum used to work,' I said, walking past her little office before taking them upstairs to where I had made the phone call to ask Emma out on our first date. It meant they could now associate real places with their mother and start to fill in the sketchy picture of what she was like.

The day after he did the drawing, Sam got up to go to school and the transformation was immediate: he looked like a different child. I told the school what the problem had been and, sure enough, he was absolutely fine there as well. But the incident shook me up because I saw how easy it was for things to start going wrong. That said, the anniversary of Emma's death came and went without incident. The day itself was spent at Damon and Georgie's house, and although I was clock-watching throughout, thinking 'Only another two hours to go', 'Only half an hour to go', when 6.26 came and went and I saw the children were busy playing, I thought, 'Phew, another year done.' I was the one who was apprehensive of the day, not them. To them, it was just another normal day, which is how I wanted it to be because it also showed me that they were progressing in the right direction, rather than getting dragged down by their mother's death.

We embarked on the third year without Emma and the first

thing I noticed was that the children were happier and stronger than ever. The Daddy chats were increasingly rare, and Molly had now taken to going straight into bored teenager mode when I asked her if she was all right. 'Yeees, okay Dad, we've done that one, change the record? I don't need a Daddy chat, I've just broken a fingernail. It's all right.'

The children also announced to me that they wanted to spend Christmas at home. They'd had two Christmases in the sun, and one with their mother just after her knee operation. It was now time to exorcise that memory and to put a new one into their collective memory bank: Christmas in our cosy new home. We had the works: the enormous tree in the big kitchen, lots of presents piled up around it, and the full Christmas dinner on the day. We didn't go shooting around the country seeing people: we just stayed at home, relaxing, seeing some family and friends. There were no wobbles from the children and indeed, by and large, I have found that, after the first year of 'anniversaries' was over, subsequent wobbles from them have tended come out of the blue, rather than on predictable occasions such as Emma's birthday or Christmas.

The children and I were by now completely at ease with bringing Emma up in the course of conversation, and they talked about her to their friends, something which they never did when she was ill, or in the first year after she died. Molly, in particular, who had used her school as a haven from what was going on at home and who had never mentioned that her mum was ill, was now happy to say to her friends, 'Oh, my mum used to like that.' Similarly, if the kids had just done something at school, a concert, or a dance show, for example, although I would sit there in the audience and think, 'God, Emma would have loved to see this,' which saddened me immensely, I still told the child in question afterwards, 'Mum would have been really proud to see you,' not as if I was about to burst into tears, but as a statement of fact, so that that child could still feel a connection to their mother and have a sense that she remained involved in what they were doing.

As for my wall of drawers, the issues that were floating around were still there but although I could feel their permanent presence around me, they no longer dominated me in quite the same way as they did before. I could now say, when a thought or memory came fluttering into view, 'Not now. I'll deal with you later on when I'm ready,' and I could finish whatever it was that I was doing, then sit down later that evening and think, 'Okay, now what was it I had to think about? Ah, yes, the time when Emma . . .' And I could address that issue, before putting it away in a drawer – until it emerged again, whenever that might be. This made me feel much more in control of the whole situation.

The fact that I could deal with this wall of issues on my terms may explain why, in May 2007, I suddenly had, for a few fleeting minutes, a true feeling of happiness. That was a monumentally important realisation. I was in Texas for work and had met up with a couple of ranchers whom I had photographed a few years back for a book I was doing on cowboys, before Emma had got ill. As I sat there sharing some beers with these guys on this country road that was like a red dust track, I was overjoyed to see them again because they had been really helpful and had become good buddies of mine, and it suddenly dawned on me that I hadn't felt this happy for years – over five years to be precise. For a brief moment, I felt fantastic: my mind was free of worry, I was as carefree as I once used to be, and I had shed the permanent sensation of my shoulders being weighed down with sorrow. For me, this was a revelation, a real ray of hope and, as Kim the bereavement counsellor had told me over 13 months before, this meant that I was very slowly beginning to heal. The feeling didn't last long, but it was an eye-opener for me that I was starting to experience sensations again that I had long ago left behind.

About a month after returning from Texas, I went to Darfur to take photographs of some of the extraordinary women who have been reduced to such harrowing circumstances in this war-ravaged part of the word. I had left Khartoum and was in the middle of the desert in a small town called Nyala, which happened to have a United Nations Population Fund house. Although it belongs to the UN, this is not a compound with bells-and-whistles security, but rather a simple house where people can come in and voice any concerns they might have to the personnel. Amazingly, it also had a WiFi satellite link, so I managed to ring home to tell the children that my mobile and laptop worked and that everything was fine (I had warned them before going away that in all likelihood I would be out of contact once I left Khartoum) and, soon after, I got a text message from Maisy. This was actually not ideal because Darfur is such a harsh and terrible place that I needed a lot of emotional energy just to get my head round what I was seeing, so I didn't really want my children contacting me and making me feel even more emotionally vulnerable than my surroundings already made me. Maisy's text simply said, 'R u going to Mum's grave on her birthday?'

I decided to reply via email. 'Yes, why?'

'Well, I'd like to come with you.'

'That's fine,' I replied. Which it was, and it was interesting that she had obviously got to the point where she wanted to do that, because she had been the one who did not want to see her mother again after visiting her in hospital in Guildford. Maisy, who looks like a carbon copy of Emma at the same age, is a sensitive little girl but incredibly strong at the same time. She is very like her mother in personality, too, and is the one in the family who is very organised and calm, both at school and at home. She'll empty the dishwasher, will prepare her packed lunch, and will prepare her clothes the night before – not because I tell her to, but simply because she likes doing that. Her decision to go and see her mother's grave was very bold, and although I could have done without her asking me when I was in Darfur, of all places ('That's classic, why couldn't she have thought to ask when I was still at home?' I remember thinking at the time), I admired the fact that she was the first one of the children to want to go. She also made it clear that she wanted it to be just the two of us who visited. That was important to her.

I got home and Emma's birthday was a couple of weeks later. On the morning, I told the other kids, 'Maisy is not going to school this morning because I'm taking her to Mum's grave.'

Molly was fine about it and didn't want to go – not that I would have taken her at the same time because of what I had promised Maisy. But, inevitably, seeing his older sister go, Sam piped up, 'I'd like to go, too, Dad.'

'Oh, you said it would just be you and me,' pleaded Maisy.

I was caught between the devil and the deep blue sea but I felt I had no choice. So I decided the only thing I could do was to take them both, drop Sam at Emma's parents' house while I took Maisy, then swap over and take Sam.

When we arrived at the grave, Maisy immediately got very upset. We were only there for five minutes, we placed one of the four roses from our rose bush on the grave and had a cuddle, but it was difficult for her to see the actual place where her mother had been laid to rest. It focused her mind on the reality of the situation and, not surprisingly, she found that distressing. When it was Sam's turn, he too placed one of the roses and got upset because I don't think he had quite realised, when he had asked to come along, what going to her grave truly meant. Like Maisy, he wasn't prepared for the emotional impact of physically seeing the piece of earth under which his mother was buried. After the event, though, they were both pleased to have gone, because they now had somewhere to focus on when they conjured up the image of Emma's grave. And I thought that their desire to go – and Molly has since said that she too would now like to visit – was a positive sign that they were starting to heal, and indicated great strength and maturity on their part. Although I don't know when they will next go, I am sure that one day they will.

A further sign that I too was gradually coming to terms with Emma's death – even though I know I will never get over it – was that around this time, I started to understand that, actually, I didn't need to have a woman around me for the sake of it. I had avoided finding myself in the situation that many widowers find themselves in, namely falling for, and marrying, the first woman who comes along and shows them some affection. I think this happens because many of them are so desperate for love and affection after what can often be several years of emotional trauma that, understandably, they are very vulnerable.

I had had several relationships with women after Emma died, some of which were very brief, but others were more serious. The children, who met a few of these women, never failed to comment on them in their typically incisive way. 'Ooh, she's nice, Dad,' Sam might say, or, as Maisy once memorably put it, 'Daddy, I don't want you to have a girlfriend right now, or at least not one like that.' Enough said – and she was right, as well. Each of these women ended up being a drain on me emotionally, through no fault of their own, simply because I wasn't ready for any sort of commitment, so I finally decided during that summer that I didn't need to search for a full-on relationship and that henceforth I would have to be totally sure about a woman before getting involved. Anyway, I reasoned, she would have a tough act to follow – Emma *was* my other half, and not many people are lucky enough to meet their true soul mate in life – so she would have to be spot on to disrupt the family life I now had with my children.

As for actually remarrying, and the children acquiring a stepmother, I am not even thinking about that at the moment. I have simply reached the stage where I think it would be nice to meet someone I could truly share my life with, because sometimes it is lonely bringing up three children, and it would be nice to share not only my passions and interests but also my worries and joys. However, I'm not actively looking for that special person because I know that it will happen in its own time. It could take me another 10 years, it might not be until Sam has left home, but what is liberating is knowing that that does not bother me. I'm quite happy to be the single guy with his kids – or the old git who lives on the hill, as I sometimes joke.

In the summer of 2007, we went on holiday to the Ardèche, in the south of France, to a wonderful campsite where the tents are in fact built like yurts, are much more comfortable than normal tents and have proper beds, so the whole experience is a notch up from normal camping. The kids love proper camping with sleeping bags on the ground, but I just felt like something a bit different for once. However, the main difference, and one that didn't really occur to me until we arrived at the campsite, was that this was the very first holiday we had gone on as a family of four where no one knew who we were, and no one knew our 'story'. I was therefore going to have to come face to face with people who would probably be wondering what this single man was doing with his three kids; no doubt their first thought would be that I had slept with the secretary, and this was my two weeks' allocated holiday time with my kids. Or that is what I assumed they would be thinking.

We arrived after a long drive down and quickly settled in for our first night under canvas, which the kids thought was great because, although it was lashing with rain outside, we were all in the same tent, so it made the whole experience much more fun. After a week, another yurt next to ours became available, so the girls moved into their own lodgings, while I stayed with Sam in a boys-only tent. That would have been fine, except that on this particular night, the Mistral wind was blowing a gale, so Sam was lying in my bed absolutely terrified by the creaking, swishing noises coming from the trees outside. Meanwhile, the two girls were in the tent next door and all was not well with them either: when I went in to investigate, I found Molly in a total panic, her foot covered in blood after picking up a huge splinter, and Maisy curled up in bed in floods of tears. Frankly, I didn't know which child to attend to first: Molly with her bloody foot, Sam who was shaking with terror because of the wind outside, or Maisy who was in floods of tears. What a time for them to fall off the perch – and all at once! I decided my priority was to patch Molly up, so I ran out into the dark to ask at the campsite office if they had any plasters, ran back, did what I could to sort Molly out, ran over to see how Sam was in my tent, then finally ran back to see Maisy.

'What's up with you?' I asked her, finally.

'I want my mummy on holiday with us,' she sobbed.

Bang! I wasn't prepared for that at all, and all I could do was give her an enormous hug and whisper to her, 'Well, we all would, Maise.' What else was there to say? For all the children, finding themselves in unfamiliar surroundings, with the trees screaming and bending above their heads, was understandably scary, and it brought home to them that their mum was not there to comfort them. However happy and strong they now were, and however relaxed they were about talking about their mother, when they were sad or scared, they still missed her. What is tough is that this will always be the case for them, as I explained to Molly on the eve of her 13th birthday. That longing for their mum will never leave them, and it is an entirely normal feeling which will spring out at them every now and again, often out of the blue, as we were starting to discover. In due course, they will eventually come to accept it, and understand that they will always be upset when it happens, even when they are grown up and have children of their own.

The next morning, the gale-force winds had abated, we woke up to a beautiful sunny day and scorching hot temperatures, and I was able to laugh about the previous night's crisis. Before long, I had got talking to the couple whose tent was next to ours, and, heading off any questions, I introduced myself and decided to explain straight away that I was on holiday with my kids and that my wife had died of cancer a few years back. 'But it's fine, we're just getting on, we're all okay.'

And the wife turned to me and said, 'You know, I can see that there's a special bond between you and your children and that you are incredibly close to them. I could immediately tell that you're not on your two-week access holiday!'

That touched me deeply because I had no idea how the outside world saw us. It wasn't as if I particularly cared, but I had long been acutely aware, at school concerts or plays, for example, that I was the only one turning up for my kids, and I did wonder whether people who didn't know us instantly jumped to the wrong conclusions about why there didn't seem to be a mother for these children.

A couple of days later, we were just getting changed after a day spent on the nearby river, when Molly suddenly appeared wearing a pair of purple tracky bottoms from The White Stuff. I did a double take because they had actually belonged to Emma and I had completely forgotten Molly had taken them when we had done the great clothes sort-out almost three years before when Emma had died, but she had obviously kept them for all that time in her chest of drawers in anticipation of the day when they would finally fit her. It felt very weird indeed seeing Molly dressed in her mother's clothes, particularly as I remembered that the last time I had seen Emma wearing those particular tracky pants was when she was already ill and was cuddled up on the sofa with the kids watching TV.

The holidays were a big success and it felt as if we were all taking another step forward in the long process of learning to live alongside our grief. Part of the rehabilitation involves not wanting to be perceived by others as a gibbering wreck just because I have lost my wife and my kids have lost their mother. We want to be perceived as normal human beings who can talk about things other than Emma and what she went through, and when you meet new people who know nothing about you, you are free to do just that, and to become once again, in my case, simply a photographer, not a man whose wife has died and who happens to be a photographer.

In the years following Emma's death, I had gradually realised that it was easy to be held back in my healing process by people who were themselves unable to move on. It was also very difficult with Emma's childhood friends, Gina, Jo and Becca, to get away from the fact that what happened to Emma united us for ever in a way which is unique but which, in the long term, can become almost unhealthy. I know they were very close to her during her illness, and it transpired that Emma told them things which she never told me, which left me having to decide whether we should discuss what was said between them and, if so, what good, if any, that would do to me. I didn't always feel they understood quite how hellish it had been for me because, understandably, they were getting Emma's version of events, and for all I know, she was complaining to them that I was being absolutely useless and unsupportive. After all, my friends had seen events unfold from my perspective, so it was logical that Emma's friends might see things from hers.

Around the time of the third anniversary of Emma's death, however, I happened to be speaking to Gina one evening and she revealed things to me that completely altered my willingness to continue discussing Emma with her, Jo and Becca. I was talking about what Emma had been like when I had taken her in for her first chemo session, and how she had been happy for me to leave her and not to hang around the ward. Gina then said that when she herself had gone in to visit Emma later that morning, Emma had got so upset that she had been forced to close the curtains round the bed. She had then completely crumbled, completely and utterly, and was beside herself with anguish. 'What am I doing here?' she kept crying. 'Will I die? I don't want to die!' and had sobbed helplessly in Gina's arms. She was in total shock at the situation she now found herself in and was obviously terrified.

I was stunned. What Gina had just disclosed was something I had never had the slightest inkling of. 'You know, she always had this fear about dying when the kids were small,' she continued, 'and she had that fear from when she and Becca were both young. She just wore a paper-thin veil to disguise her fear the whole time that she was ill. Talk to Becca about it.'

I got straight on the phone to Becca who confirmed this. 'Yes, as far back as her late teens. All Emma wanted was to have kids and to have them young, like her mother and grandmother had done. But her biggest fear, and one which she regularly voiced, was "What if I die when my children are small?" So she always had that fear. Always.'

235

How strange that was for Emma to have been afraid of this before she had even had a serious boyfriend, especially as there was no history in her family of women dying young and leaving children behind. We were married for 15 years and had a great marriage: despite the usual tension and bickering which occurs between people who have been together for that length of time, I felt we had a very close relationship. Of course, as many mothers do, she would occasionally snap and say, 'God, can you imagine if I die now, how on earth would you cope?' But what was truly shocking for me was discovering that she had been saying that since she was 16 or 17 and that her worst fear in life had *always* been dying when her kids were young. It was a terrible thing to find out, and inevitably, it forced me to decide whether or not I wanted to lift the lid on a potentially enormous can of worms. Did I want to find out what else Emma may have said to her friends? And then, why stop there? Why not quiz her parents about what Emma had told them? And what about the priest at the hospice whom she saw on a couple of occasions: what fears did she expose to him?

It was now clear that, unbeknown to me, she had had moments when she feared she was going to die, whereas other than the occasion when she was sitting on the bathroom floor and acknowledged the possibility that this thing *might* get her, she never once admitted to me that she was going to die. Never ever. I now had to ask myself why? Why had she never wanted to tell me?

I believe she kept those fears away from me for a variety of reasons. Firstly, her friends already knew of her fears about dying young, so it would have come as no surprise to them that Emma voiced them again during her illness. Best friends disclose things to each other that often they don't even tell their partners, and as these friends had Emma's best interests at heart, she would have felt safe telling them whatever was on her mind. Secondly, people instinctively want to protect those they love the most, and that usually means their parents, their partner and their children, so for Emma, she wanted to protect us from her biggest fear. As I discovered from her diary, she obviously felt intensely guilty, worried and sad for what her illness was doing to our family unit, so she couldn't bear the idea of burdening us, on top of that, with her fear of dying. Also, if she thought I knew what she was thinking, then how could I stay strong for her? And as, throughout our marriage, she had gained strength from me staying positive, she could not afford for me to be weighed down by the mental strain of coping with her anguish because she would then fold emotionally as well. Worst of all, if our children became aware of the situation, then she probably thought we would all end up sinking together. Emma was desperate to live, and terrified of dying. She absolutely did not want to capitulate, which is why she fought as hard as she possibly could until the very end. So it's quite possible that Emma reasoned that 'If I mention this to Jon, he's going to go off at the deep end, and that's really not what I need right now. I need someone to be strong for me, and to give me love and affection'. Because the final sting in the tail of what Gina told me, and the revelation which arguably was the most difficult for me to comprehend, was that Emma had once told her during her illness that she didn't think I was cuddling her enough. There was no point in arguing the opposite, even though I know what really happened, because Gina doesn't know what went on behind closed doors. She doesn't know about all the times I would get into bed and gently lay my hand on Emma, in an attempt to say, 'I'm here, I'm still here, I want to reassure you,' and she would immediately become livid. 'Can't you see I'm trying to sleep! Why are you touching me, you know I need all the sleep I can get!' It was at that point in my conversation with Gina that I decided to stop, to walk away from this can of worms, because I would gain nothing from delving any deeper.

I am in awe of Emma's immense strength in keeping her biggest fear in life from me for all those years and especially during her final illness. And I feel no guilt for not knowing about it. Emma had her reasons for not confiding in me, and I think I know what they are. But if I start going down the route of trying to find out what else she may have kept from me, or what she may have told other people, I am sure it will drive me slowly towards insanity. Or at least towards a state of perpetual torment. And I believe that serves no purpose. I have now decided to let go of all those 'what if' questions, and have since told Gina, Jo and Becca that I never again want to discuss the 14-month period when Emma was dying.

16

Now We Are Four

I KNOW I wasn't the perfect husband or carer, and Emma wasn't the perfect wife or patient. But that's the reality, because this illness tests relationships in a way in which everyday life rarely requires them to be tested. I had been shocked and hurt to find out from Emma's girlfriends that allegedly I hadn't cuddled her enough, or that I hadn't known about her fear of dying young. When, around the same time, another of our friends also informed me that, during the spring of 2004 when Emma was 'better', she felt that I was being emotionally pushed away by my wife, I realised if I wanted to preserve my sanity I not only had to stop talking about Emma's illness with those who had witnessed it , but I also had to realise that truth is not absolute: it is relative and personal. And each of these people believed that they knew the truth of the situation, even if they only dipped in and out of it, whereas I, who was steeped in it on a permanent basis, had a far more accurate version of what was going on. Furthermore, Emma was no longer here to defend herself against any of her actions or words, or to give her version of what truly happened and what she truly felt, and it was unfair to her memory and to what she had had to endure to hold up certain things she may have said in moments of bleak despair, and to assert, 'That's what she thought of you, Jon,' or 'That's what she was feeling during the whole of her illness.' I don't need to know what Emma thought of me in her darkest hour; nor do I need to know what she may have said to someone once, in a moment that could be taken entirely out of context if that person to whom she spoke didn't know what else had gone on that day or that week. There's enough sadness as it is in my life just trying to cope with Emma's death without adding to it unnecessarily by being told distorted truths – albeit without any intention of malice – by others. Importantly, too, my children have enough to deal with without being bombarded by confusing and potentially upsetting versions of what their mother may or may not have said or thought. Everyone's memory is selective but I happen to believe that mine is inevitably more accurate than those who were on the periphery of what was happening to Emma. As a result, my recollection of events is the one I would like to pass on to my children.

I know what happened between us, and I know that I can't go back and make it better, because that is no longer possible. This illness was so vicious that it warped our relationship for ever. The fact was, the basis on which we fell in love, got married and had children, had gone, and gone for good, because it was clear we were *never* going to return to how we had been, even if Emma had survived. I sometimes felt as if I was teetering on the edge of a cliff and that I might fall off at any moment, because not only was the cancer eating away at Emma but it was eating away at our relationship and in such an awful way that I didn't know how much more I could take. The unimaginable strain this barbaric illness had put on us meant that at times I hated her for what it had done to us and for the fact that she was going to be deserting us: it was almost as if her death was a betrayal of her love for us, and that is what angered me so much. Several times – not just after the row at Sarah's, but after she had finished her chemo and was in a really fragile mental state – she had turned round to me and aggressively shouted, 'You want me dead, don't you? You'd be better off with me dead, wouldn't you?' and I would be thinking to myself, 'Well, actually, whilst you're like this, yes. That would be the best solution. Because it's going to happen anyway.' And I am absolutely sure that I am not the only person in a similar situation to have reasoned like this; equally, if someone has never lived through what I did, they don't know that it's actually a normal thought to have.

So do I feel guilty for thinking those things? Absolutely not. Nor do I feel guilty for deciding to let go of all the 'what if's, and of the things that were left unsaid between us because Emma never accepted she was going to die. Because holding on to these things stops me and therefore my children from continuing down our path of healing and from being able to live alongside our grief so that it no longer consumes us but simply becomes a part of what we are now. For that reason, too, I do not feel guilty about letting go of my relationship with Emma. I will always love her, and I am fortunate that I am now able to have good memories of her and of our times together, as opposed to the falsely jolly memories I would conjure up for the children in the first couple of years after her death in an attempt to keep their rapidly evaporating memory banks as full as possible. I am exceptionally fortunate to have had those years with her, but I am not betraying our love by being attracted to, and having relationships with, other women.

It often takes an event as big as this to make people see their life with greater clarity and to make them realise who they want to keep in their life and who they don't. After what I went through, there was an inescapable fall-out in terms of friendships. I learned things about myself and about other people which were invaluable and now that I have pared my previous friendships down to those people I do still want to stay in contact with, I can see with excitement how young shoots of new friendships are beginning to spring up when I meet new people, people who know nothing about my previous life and who take me for who I am, not for poor Jon, whose wife died, leaving him with three kids. It's a great feeling for me to know that things are improving and that I will meet new people – even if sometimes I still have to force myself to go out, often egged on by Molly ('You've been invited, Dad, so it's really rude not to go') – because it means I'm on the up, I'm out of the worst period of deep mourning.

In some ways, I have changed how I see the world since Emma died and consciously try to find the beauty in it. Whereas previously, when I was covering a difficult subject for my work, I would aim to make the photographs as shocking as possible, now I search out the beauty, as I did when I went to Darfur: these women's lives are awful beyond description, yet they possess an extraordinary inner beauty which I was determined to convey through my lens.

I also try to laugh and smile more, even smiling at people I don't know, at the risk of them thinking I am either mad or trying it on with them. I try to help those who have problems in their lives more than I used to, and more than just hearing, I try and remember to listen to what people are actually telling me. I do still have days when I inexplicably feel very low, but I have learned that, in time, the feeling will pass. And it's also important for me to search out situations which give me pleasure or to rediscover those things which used to make me feel good, such as going out on the water with my surfboard for a couple of hours and feeling exhilarated by the open space and the waves, because I had forgotten what those sensations were or would simply say to myself, 'Oh, I'll go out tomorrow,' and then not do it. I try harder to seize the moment and not to let it slip by. And, since my experience in Texas with my cowboy friends, I have found myself really laughing freely on a couple more occasions, and they were real eye-openers because I realised that deep happiness was now tangible, it was not too far away. I could finally start, very gently, to let the handbrake off, and to look forward to enjoying the ride again.

One of the other signs that I am starting to find some level of peace is that I have decided to pursue a search that I was about to embark on when Emma got ill: I have decided to search for my birth mother and father. My adoptive dad died when I was 17, I have a limited, arms-length relationship with my adoptive mother, and deep down, I know that I need to know who my natural parents are, because that represents perhaps the final stage in my desire to clarify my life and to rid it, where possible, of any elements which cause me unnecessary stress.

I know very few details about my natural parents: I know that they were both medical students and that my father is French Canadian, which means he probably no longer lives in the UK. I was adopted when I was two days old and, in the same way that I think about what happened to Emma every single day, I imagine that hardly a day goes by when my birth mother doesn't think about the baby she gave away, and doesn't wonder what became of him and what sort of life he went on to have. As a parent myself, it would be inconceivable to forget about such a child for more than a few hours at a stretch, so, whoever she is, I think it's time I found the woman who gave birth to me. What's more, Emma had wanted me to find her, and the children now want me to do so too: Sam even announces to people, 'Do you know, my dad is half French Canadian?'! So I now feel that this search, which would have been impossible for me to contemplate even a year ago, is very much the next thing I have to do if I am to get on with the next stage of my life, and although I have no idea where it will lead me, as Neil Young once said in an interview, I will 'open the door and let the wind blow through'.

What about my own children? How do I see their lives evolving? Their own mother, Emma, had wanted nothing more than to dedicate her life to them, yet was prevented from doing so by a cruel, random illness. But in the short years they had with her, these children had the most incredible, loving start that any child could wish for and, for that, I believe they are fortunate indeed. The fact that Emma did not leave behind memory boxes – as terminally ill parents with young children are often encouraged to do – is of no importance to them because they are surrounded by reminders of her: without turning our house into a shrine, there is evidence of her presence in every room in the form of photographs of her with the children, mugs that say 'Emma' on them, household items which she bought, and cards that she sent or received. We talk about her the whole time, and people who meet us immediately realise that nothing is taboo when it comes to Emma, and that this openness has contributed to the children's strength and happiness.

As for how each child is growing up, Molly most resembles me in terms of personality and, while she can be impetuous and emotional, she also has a great imagination and sense of humour and is very loyal to her friends. Being the oldest, when her mother became ill, she took the lead in terms of being supportive and protective of her siblings and, to a certain extent, of me and, despite Emma's death, she remains a very positive person who doesn't dwell on negative situations, which I think will stand her in good stead in the future.

She also has a maturity beyond her years, as does Maisy who was deeply affected by Emma's illness. Whenever she visited her mother in hospital, she would just get on the bed and cuddle up to her, which was why seeing her lying in a coma in Guildford distressed her so much that she never saw her mother again. That is a terrible experience for a child to have to come to terms with, but all along Maisy was the one who decided how to handle the situation and, of course, was the first of the children to want to visit Emma's grave. Apart from sharing her mother's personality, the two of them are so alike physically that in photographs of Emma at Maisy's age, it's actually quite difficult to tell them apart. Her quiet sense of organisation – I hear her clattering around with the lunchboxes in the morning before I have even got up – and her sensitivity mask an incredibly strong little girl who refuses to take any crap from anyone.

Sam, being the youngest, has probably had the most to deal with. For him to make sense of what has happened in his short life is undoubtedly difficult but he is a very bubbly little boy with a great sense of what the world is about – an awareness that, once again, very much belies his young age. He has had to fight to remember his mother and likes nothing better now than to chat and reminisce about her. He is growing up strong and active but also loves a big hug, as do the two girls, and indeed I make sure there is plenty of hugging and cuddling between all four of us, because I am a firm believer that physical contact is vital for children's emotional well-being.

What I hope is that all three children will grow into the adults that they were going to be if Emma had lived. Or rather, that her death will shape them into almost identical but slightly better, more rounded versions of what they would have been. They are undoubtedly more emotionally aware than their peers and are already quite philosophical about minor accidents in life, such as falling off the trampoline or their bike, or having the odd sore throat. As a result of this horrible thing which happened to them when they were far too young, they will be able to prioritise the various upsets that they will inevitably encounter as they go through life. After all, God willing, there won't be anything worse in life than losing their mother when they did. So when they don't get the job they want, or they break up with a partner, they might be able to think to themselves, 'Ah yes, but I survived my mum's death, so I'll survive this.' And ultimately, I hope that will make them stronger and more fearless as a result, because they can be confident about facing whatever life has to offer them. So they didn't get that job, or that relationship came to an end? Not great. But no one died. Sadly, it's not a bad thing for them that they will be able to rationalise such downturns and, whilst I wouldn't wish what happened to my kids to happen to anyone else's, it seems to me that people who have grown up with a cloudless childhood are not always able to cope when difficulties arise.

When you are about to have a first child, you read books, listen to other parents and try to prepare yourself for what will happen when that baby is born. The minute you become a parent, of course, you realise that nobody or nothing actually prepares you for what it is like to have a baby. The same happens with death. Nobody can prepare you for the grief and for what you will go through when somebody close to you dies. No words can diminish the pain or reduce the time it takes for it to become less raw and all-consuming. Any healing that takes place will occur in its own time and will come about as a result of what *you* decide to do, not others. The children and I went through what we did together, as a unit, and, as result, we now have an incredible and unique bond, the sort that is only created when a group of people have been through something as truly awful as we did. I have seen this in parts of the world where people have endured appalling situations, so it's not just the preserve of terminal illness. But the extraordinary common ground that we now have, the way in which we understand each other so well, will be a real strength for us in years to come.

Nowadays, I can finally smile because, although I know there is still a long way to go for all four of us, I can see that we are once more fully able to enjoy life. I know that my children are going to be fine, and I think Emma can see that from wherever she is. She can look down on us and see that I did it: not only am I coping, I am also bringing the children up as much as possible as she would have done, and bringing them up to be happy, balanced people. No, their lives are not the same as if their mother was alive. But their lives are not worse – just different. And I hope she can rest easy with that knowledge.

From *'I'll See You In My Dreams'*

Tho' the days are long, twilight sings a song,
Of the happiness that used to be.
Soon my eyes will close,
Soon I'll find repose
And in dreams you're always near to me.
I'll see you in my dreams,
Hold you in my dreams.
Someone took you out of my arms.
Still I feel the thrill of your charms,
Lips that once were mine,
Tender eyes that shine,
They will light my way tonight,
I'll see you in my dreams.

(Copyright Gus Khan/Isham Jones, and memorably sung by
Joe Brown at the Concert for George which I attended, in
memory of George Harrison)

Acknowledgements

I would like to thank:

All those who helped us out during our stormy days, especially the medical teams: Dr Jeremy Whelan and all his team at the Middlesex Hospital (that was), London; Mr Stephen Cannon and his team at the Royal National Orthopaedic Hospital, Stanmore; Dr Whittaker and everybody at the Royal Surrey County Hospital, Guildford; Dr Peter Hargreaves and all the wonderful staff at the Macmillan Unit (that was) at the King Edward VII Hospital, Midhurst.

Friends and family who did and still do offer practical help and support.

Clare Hulton at Vermilion for getting this off the ground and seeing the importance of this story. David Luxton, my agent.

Finally Debbie Beckerman, for writing this book with me and understanding the ups and downs involved in recounting these events and emotions.